Corporal John Tough, a member of the 1st Northumberland (Berwick) Battalion Home Guard sights his rifle in the shelter of a boat at Lindisfarne, June 30, 1942. (Historic Military Press)

ACKNOWLEDGMENT: The editorial team would like to thank Robert Mitchell for his assistance with the images in this publication, as well as James Luto, Austin J. Ruddy, Arthur Ward, Mrs Mary Taylor, and, in particular, Richard Hunt (www.sussexhomeguard.co.uk) for permitting access to their collections. Colourisation of main cover image by ColourbyRJM.

Editor: John Grehan
Design: Dan Jarman
Publisher: Mark Elliott
Chief Publishing Officer: Jonathan Jackson
Senior Editor, Bookazines: Roger Mortimer
Chief Finance Officer: Nigel Cronin
Head of Production: Janet Watkins
Group CEO: Adrian Cox

Contacts
Key Publishing Ltd, PO Box 100,
Stamford, Lincolnshire, PE9 1XQ
E-mail: enquiries@keypublishing.com
www.keypublishing.com

Distribution: Seymour Distribution Ltd. Tel: 020 7429400
Printed by Precision Colour Printing Ltd, Haldane, Halesfield 1, Telford, Shropshire. TF7 4QQ

Published by Key Publishing Ltd.
www.britainatwar.com

Churchill' Home Guard

GW00500269

The news was devastating. Hitler's panzers had raced across the Ardennes and had broken through French defences on the River Meuse. Just four days after the start of the invasion of France and the Low Countries, it was evident that the British Expeditionary Force and the French armies were in an increasingly perilous position – and if France fell, Britain might be next.

There was widespread concern that with its soldiers fighting for their lives across the Channel, Britain had been left unprotected and defenceless. The great fear was that the German parachutists would land in the UK to dislocate the war effort and, ultimately, to prepare the way for invasion. So, on the evening of May 14, 1940, Anthony Eden, the Secretary of State for War, delivered a broadcast calling for British subjects to enrol in a new formation to be called the Local Defence Volunteers. That name was soon to change, becoming the Home Guard.

The Government had expected 150,000 people to volunteer. By the end of May almost 400,000 had put their names down to join what would become a vast military organisation, a force which undertook a huge number of vital tasks that otherwise would have tied down the regular army. In this detailed study, we look at the enormous contribution made by the Home Guard in terms of manning anti-aircraft batteries and defending the coastline. We examine the weapons employed by the Home Guard, including the Blacker Bombard and Northover Projector.

We take a journey back in time to that summer of 1940, when the threat of invasion seemed so frighteningly real. This was never more so than on September 7, when the codeword *Cromwell* was issued by the Chiefs of Staff. Meaning 'invasion imminent', this resulted in many Home Guard units rushing into action, destroying bridges, shooting at passing cars and laying impromptu minefields! Packed with an unrivalled collection of photographs, this is the story of the real Home Guard.

John Grehan

John Grehan
Editor

82

A 'then and now' picture of Sergeant Lord Strabolgi, in charge of No.3 Section of the Palace of Westminster Home Guard, leading his men on patrol, March 1942. Commanded by Major Robert Grimston M.P., the unit was formed by members of both houses, official members of various staffs in the buildings, and members of the press.
(Historic Military Press/image by Robert Mitchell)

Contents

31

64

24

37

'This Country is at War with Germany'

On September 3, 1939, Prime Minister Neville Chamberlain delivered his stark statement to the people of the United Kingdom, ending with the chilling words "I know that you will all play your part with calmness and courage".

Barbed wire laid out in Parliament Square, near Big Ben and the Palace of Westminster, following the declaration of war in September 1939. (NARA)

The nation held its breath. Everyone in the country waited for the announcement. At 11.15 hours on September 3, 1939, a profound silence descended upon every home in the land as men, women and children gathered round the wireless. The music stopped and the thin voice of the Prime Minister, Neville Chamberlain, speaking from the Cabinet Room at 10 Downing Street, uttered the memorable words: "This country is at war with Germany."

No one knew what it would mean for them or their families. The invasion of Poland, over which Britain and France had declared war against Germany, seemed such a remote event, but already the fear of German bombers blackening the sky had created a mood of national anxiety. Preparations had been in hand for some time, with blackout precautions in force and the likes of schools and public swimming baths having been prepared to accept mass casualties, from where the bodies would be taken in cardboard boxes to their lime-pit graves. After all, people were told, the bomber would always get through.

Though still a child at the time, Dorothy Williams recalled that momentous day all too clearly: "My parents followed the events very closely, so when we knew that war could break out – I think it was 11 o'clock in the morning – we were really keyed up. I was frightened. We didn't know what was ahead… Father said that if the Germans ever landed, he would kill us all rather than us ever fall into their hands. That frightened us a little bit too… Oh yes, he meant it. He had been right through the previous war and he had seen a lot."[1]

Two days earlier Operation *Pied Piper* had started, under which eventually 3.5 million women and children were relocated from what were considered to be high-risk urban areas to the countryside, distant coastal

ABOVE: A newspaper seller announces the declaration of war against Germany on September 3, 1939. (Historic Military Press)

towns and even the highlands. Sanitoriums had released thousands of tuberculosis patients to free their beds for the bomb-blast casualties. Measures were even in place for Regional Controllers to govern the country after Whitehall and Westminster had been bombed into oblivion.

Those with money, as in all times, used their wealth to their advantage and took themselves off to safer regions without waiting for government assistance or intervention. It was reported at Southampton that 5,000 people left for the USA in just two days, whilst those who

could afford their own transport headed, in some cases quite literally, for the hills. Constantine Fitzgibbon wrote of this exodus of the affluent: "A constant stream of private cars and London taxis driving up to his mother's front door in the Thames valley in the September of '39, filled with men and women of all ages and in various stages of hunger, exhaustion and fear, offering absurd sums for accommodation in her already overcrowded house, and even for food. This horde of satin-clad, pin-striped refugees poured through for two or three days, eating everything that was for sale, downing all the spirits of the pubs, and then vanished."[2]

Of course, hotel proprietors in the districts far removed from the urban sprawl of London, Manchester, Liverpool, Portsmouth, Sheffield, Sunderland and Birmingham were quick to take advantage

ABOVE: Civilians heading for cover on September 3, 1939. As the sirens sounded across London for the first time, at 11.27 hours that day, people immediately made their way to the shelters. The original caption states: "Without fuss, even with smiles, and with curiosity as to what would happen next rather than fear, the people made for the shelters which were already in being. There was confidence that our defences were in good order. The little group [seen here]... was snapped in Whitehall on the morning of September 3rd." (Historic Military Press)

of people's fears, blatantly advertising the security of their locations in the newspapers – some had even taken reservations as early as February that year. "Everywhere houses were being closed, furniture stored, children transported, servant dismissed, lawns ploughed, dower houses and shooting lodges crammed to capacity; mother-in-arms and nannies were everywhere gaining control," noted one writer. "Everywhere little groups of close friends were arranging to spend the war together."[3] »

ABOVE: Preparations for war underway as gas masks are distributed to Britain's population. Dated October 9, 1938, the original caption states that this image shows "London's sandwich-men appealing to the people to be fitted for gas masks". (Historic Military Press)

ABOVE: A crowd gathers in Parliament Square, London, anxious to learn what steps the British government would take following the German invasion of Poland. Taken on Saturday, September 2, 1939, the grainy appearance of this photograph is because it is an example of a "radiophoto". So rapidly were pictures such as this transmitted across the Atlantic that they were printed in newspapers and journals across the United States on September 3, 1939. (Historic Military Press)

longer confined to the battlefield." He warned his people that they should be ready "for whatever service or sacrifice it may demand".

A CALL TO ARMS

During the Munich Crisis of September 1938, when Europe teetered on the brink of war, more than 500,000 people had enrolled in the Air Raid Precautions (ARP) services, while others had joined the Royal Air Force Voluntary Reserve or the Territorial Army. In May 1939, conscription was introduced in the form of the Military Training Act, but this called only for young men between the ages of twenty and twenty-one to undertake six months military training. On the declaration of war, however, parliament passed the National Service (Armed Forces) Act under which men between the ages of eighteen to forty-one could be called up for active service.

The government, though, was cautious with its implementation of conscription. In the First World War, many factories, workshops and offices had seen large numbers of its workers rushing to join up, leaving a huge manpower and skills shortage.

The mass evacuations were not just simply driven by fear but were also a military necessity. If the armed forces were to be called upon to defend their cities, they did not want hordes of terrified citizens impeding their efforts. Nor did the authorities want to be deluged with thousands of civilian casualties occupying the hospital beds needed for the military.

National treasures were also on their way from the museums and galleries of the capital to be hidden deep in a Welsh quarry, among other sites. Even Billingsgate Fish Market swam with the tide, dispersing across the country.

Barrage balloons floated high above cities, their bloated bodies frowning menacingly upon nervous citizens whom Winston Churchill had warned might find themselves wandering homeless around the debris of the bomb-ravaged streets. Soldiers and police stood guard over key installations, bridges and tunnels, with camouflage adorning the more obvious structures.

On that first evening of war, the King added sombre tones to the already darkened mood. "In this grave hour perhaps the most fateful in our history," he told the nation in a BBC broadcast at 18.00 hours. "There may be dark days ahead and war is no

ABOVE: Hitler's push for *Lebensraum*, or living space, begins as German troops advance towards Warsaw following the invasion of Poland on September 1, 1939. (National Museum of the US Navy)

"When we knew that war could break out – I think it was 11 o'clock in the morning – we were really keyed up."

BELOW: Polish cavalry in action during the German invasion of their country in September 1939. Some sources state that the image was taken in or near the city of Sochaczew. (Courtesy of Marek Tuszyński)

ABOVE: On the very day that the United Kingdom declared war on Germany, the first ship to be sunk by the enemy, the SS *Athenia*, was hit by a torpedo fired by *U-30*. The original caption to this picture taken that day notes that it "shows officers of the British liner *Athenia* watching their ship sink from a deck of the *Knute Nelson*". (Historic Military Press)

Women, of course, gradually filled the vacant places, but this was not a rapid process, and the troops at the front were hampered by a shortage of many necessary items – the "shell scandal" of 1915 had not been forgotten.

The first group of men to be registered for National Service were those in the twenty to twenty-three age range in October and it was not until May 1940 that registration was extended to men aged twenty-seven. Those medically unfit were exempted, as were others in vital industries and jobs such as baking, farming, medicine, and engineering. Employers could also ask for the "deferment" of key workers and individuals could request postponement on the grounds of severe personal hardship. Hundreds of thousands of such claims were accepted by the Military Service Tribunals set up to consider such cases. Conscientious objectors also had to appear before such tribunals to argue their reasons for refusing to join-up. If their cases were not dismissed, they were granted one of several categories of exemption, and were given non-combatant jobs.

Some men did not wait to be conscripted, volunteering to join the armed forces, but this was not on the scale of the First World War, nor was there the nationalistic jingoism which had impelled young men to volunteer in their tens of thousands upon the declaration of war in 1914. Whatever glory men believed battle had to offer had long since faded in the No Man's Land of the Somme and been finally trodden underfoot in the Flanders' mud. There was, though, still some pride in wearing a uniform, and the prospect of adventure and escape from the dull poverty of life that was the lot of so many in 1930s Britain certainly had its appeal.

ABOVE: An injured survivor from SS *Athenia* is helped ashore from a rescue ship, possibly the Norwegian steamer *Knute Nelson*, at Galway Harbour. A total of 117 passengers and crew lost their lives in the liner's sinking. (Historic Military Press)

Women were not subject to conscription in any form at this stage of the war, as would be the case later. Yet, before the end of 1939, there were 43,000 individuals in the ranks of the Women's Auxiliary Air Force, the Auxiliary Territorial Service, and the Women's Royal Navy Service.

DEFENCE OF THE REALM

Despite the warnings and the threats, enemy bombs did not screech down from the skies that first autumn of the war and one of the ironies of those early months was that the first casualties of the conflict resulted from the precautions put in place in defence of the German bombers. The Air Ministry had calculated that the UK would suffer night-time bombing raids and so had imposed black-out regulations from September 1. These rules required that all windows and doors should be covered at night with suitable material such as heavy curtains, cardboard or paint, to prevent the escape of any glimmer of light that might aid enemy aircraft. Traffic lights and vehicle headlights were fitted with slotted covers to deflect their beams downwards to the ground. The blackout was enforced by civilian ARP wardens, along with the Police, who would ensure that no buildings allowed the slightest peek or glow of light. Offenders were liable to stringent legal penalties.

This measure was intended to make targeting difficult for German aircrews, but it also made movement on the ground at night hazardous. By the end of the first month of war there had been 1,130 road deaths attributed to the blackout.

These regulations were strictly enforced, as a case at Clerkenwell Police Court on September 5 shows: "William Hance, who said he was 83, was fined 40s. when charged under the Defence **»**

"WITHOUT WARNING"

NIGHT, ——
and a thousand souls lay wrapped
In sleep 'neath the quiet stars,
Glad at last that they had escaped
From wars and rumours of wars.

When—Crash!
        and a gallant ship went down
Without warning of voice or hand—
Another proof that a Nazi's pledge
Is written on shifting sand.

Allan Junior.

" S.S. ATHENIA "—Donaldson Atlantic Liner, 13,581 tons, carrying 1,720 passengers and crew outward bound for Canada, torpedoed Sept. 3, at 9.30 p.m., 200 miles west of the Hebrides. 75% of the passengers were women and children.

ABOVE: A commercially produced postcard that commemorates the sinking of SS *Athenia* on September 3, 1939. (Historic Military Press)

ABOVE: Members of the public watch as an anti-aircraft gun crew goes through its paces in London's Hyde Park on the eve of war in the summer of 1939. (NARA)

ABOVE: A part of the UK's pre-war balloon barrage falls in flames at Stanmore, Middlesex, in early 1939. The original caption, dated February 27 that year, states: "A balloon belonging to London's anti-air raid Balloon Barrage was set on fire by lightning during a freak storm. The driver of the lorry to which the balloon was attached by a steel cable felt the shock as the lightning struck his balloon. He saw it burst into flames and realised that it was likely to fall near two other balloons moored on the ground. He started up his lorry and dragged the balloon as far from them as he could. The blazing balloon crashed on top of a hangar, but the other balloons were saved." (Historic Military Press)

Regulations with displaying a light at this address in Highgate Road, Kentish Town, which was visible from outside the building. He was also charged with wilfully obstructing Police Constable Taylor in the execution of his duty. He pleaded 'Not Guilty'.

"Police constable Taylor said he went to Highgate Road at 10.25 p.m. yesterday and found a large crowd assembled. It was very hostile, and people were shouting 'Smash the door down!' In two front ground-floor rooms electric lights were on, with only a thin curtain over the window, and witness knocked at the door, which was opened by Hance. Asked to shade the lights, he refused to do so, and witness entered the house and turned off the lights. The prisoner switched them on again. 'Owing to the crowd being so

hostile I was forced to take him into custody,' added the officer." Hance was warned by Magistrate Broderick that he had got off lightly, as he might have received the full sentence of three months' imprisonment or a fine of up to £100.[4]

The blackout and the National Service Act had come into force by virtue of the Emergency Powers (Defence) Act 1939, which enabled the British Government to take up emergency powers to prosecute the war effectively. The act gave the government very wide, and unquestionably very arbitrary, powers – such as being able to take "possession or control… of any property or undertaking", permitted the "acquisition, on behalf of His Majesty, of any property other than land", and authorised the "entering and searching of any premises". The act

ABOVE: Nurses digging a trench, as part of the air raid precautions, at Guy's Hospital on August 28, 1939. (Historic Military Press)

also made provision for the "apprehension, trial, and punishment of persons offending against the Regulations and for the detention of persons whose detention appears to the Secretary of State to be expedient in the interests of the public safety or the defence of the realm." These measures were extended to include Britain's overseas territories.[5]

OFF TO WAR

Though all of the above might seem to be a disproportionate over-exaggeration of the dangers Britain faced, the war was a reality and its army, in the form of the British Expeditionary Force (BEF), was already on the move to the front line on France's eastern border. Ahead of the troops, were sent units of the Docks and Transportation services and within forty-eight hours of arriving at the French ports, these men who, in the main, had been recruited from port authorities around Britain, had the berths allocated to the BEF operating at maximum capacity.

ABOVE: RAF personnel raise a balloon barrage during the Second World War. Barrage balloon units played an important part in the UK's pre-war preparations for defence against German aircraft. (Historic Military Press)

BELOW: Britain at war. A group of soldiers head in one direction, whilst a party of evacuees head the other way, at Waterloo Station during the winter of 1939-1940. (Historic Military Press)

As the troops landed, they were passed rapidly through transit camps and their vehicles were cleared at once to Vehicle Marshalling Parks, from where they were despatched in convoys, while the troops themselves left by rail on the same day as they marched off the ships.

France's main line of defence was, of course, the famous Maginot Line, but this massive fortification ended at the border with Belgium. This tiny nation, squeezed unenviably between France and Germany, was determined to remain neutral. France had no wish to place a barrier between itself and French-speaking Wallonia and the Belgians feared that replicating the Maginot Line along its eastern border would be seen by the Germans as an act of aggression. Therefore, the northern stretch of France's frontier was ill-defended, and it was to this section of its border that the BEF was sent. Once there, the men immediately began to prepare defensive positions.

With the Germans seemingly showing no sign of risking an attack upon France or Belgium, this was the start of the "Phoney War", the "Bore War" or "Sitzkreig", as it was variously called. As the months passed by with no indication of movement by the enemy, discussions were even held about reducing the strength of the BEF and transferring the troops to other theatres where they would be of more use. Bored though the British were, they were not allowed to be idle during their time on the Belgian border and by early May 1940, more than 400 concrete pill-boxes of varying size had been completed with over 100 more under construction, while work on the improvement of field defences, barbed-wire and other obstacles proceeded continuously.

Most of the French divisions adjacent to the BEF were no more gainfully employed than their British counterparts, with nothing other than the construction of fieldworks to occupy them. It was only those men positioned along the Saar front, ahead of the Maginot Line, who came into contact with the enemy. Engagements between the French and the Germans were infrequent, and few risks were taken by either side, the troops being quite content to stay safely within their own lines. Nevertheless, there were calls for the British troops to take their share of the limited fighting on the Saar and in response to this call, the first of a number of British brigade's took up positions on the Maginot Line on November 27, 1939. It was there that the British Army suffered its first battle casualties of the war, and its solders earned their first gallantry medals.

DRINKING FOR YOUR COUNTRY

As the first few days, weeks and even months passed with the UK having been spared the onslaught so many had predicted, the mood generally began to lighten, though times were still tough for much of the population. Unemployment was still high following the world-wide Depression of the 1930s, and the emergency budget of September 27, 1939 sought to prevent an escalation of prices normally associated with wartime which would have a particularly devastating effect upon the poor. Nevertheless, taxes had to rise to pay for the war effort.

The standard rate of income tax was to rise from 5s. 6d to 7s 6d in the pound. This, though, did not affect the poor. The average weekly adult male wage, as stated in Parliament in June 1938, was 34s 9d, which equates to less than £100 per year.[6] As the personal tax allowance was, at that date, £180 per annum, most working-class people did not pay income tax. They were hit, nevertheless, with an increase of 1d on a pint of beer, 1s 3d on a bottle of whisky, 2 shillings on a pound of tobacco and 1d on a pound of sugar. »

ABOVE: Sweeping eastwards, German military vehicles pass over a bridge constructed over the Vistula River near Bydgoszcz, Poland, on September 16, 1939. (Everett Historical/Shutterstock)

ABOVE: Troops from the 51st (Highland) Division pass over a drawbridge into Fort de Sainghin on the Franco-Belgian frontier, November 3, 1939. Though the original caption claims that this shows British troops on the Maginot Line, this is in fact not correct. Built in 1878, Fort de Sainghin was occupied by a garrison and armed with forty-four guns until it was overrun by the Germans in 1914. After the First World War it served as an ammunition depot and did not form part of the Maginot Line. (Everett Historical/Shutterstock)

There were added taxes for companies which benefited directly from the war, their excess profits being subjected to sixty per cent tax. This helped pay for subsidies the government gave to essential commodities such as bread, flour, meat and milk.

The effects of the added taxation on alcohol were quickly used to justify greater consumption, a popular argument being that, "if I buy three Savings Certificates as 15s each, the State will have to pay me interest and eventually repay my capital. If, instead, I buy three bottles of whisky [then costing about 15s per bottle] I at once make an outright contribution to the government of about 29s."[7]

The brewing trade made similar pronouncements. In an editorial, the *Brewers' Journal* claimed that beer tax was expected to yield the Chancellor £256,000 a day, which, as the daily cost of the war was £6,000,000,

ABOVE: Released to the press in March 1940, this photograph shows the ascent of a barrage balloon from a barge anchored on the Thames. (Historic Military Press)

equated to one serviceman in every twenty-four being equipped, fed and paid, and one aircraft in every twenty-four being built, all at the beer drinker's expense.[8] Teetotallers were clearly not doing 'their bit'!

As 1939 passed into 1940 without undue cause for concern, increasing numbers began to return to their homes. Already many children had been allowed to return, and schools that had closed in September had been permitted to open again as early as November. But the war, which had been pursued mostly at sea as far as the UK was concerned, took a sudden lurch forward.

In March 1940, in a move intended principally to stop the export of iron ore from Sweden to Germany, which was vital to Germany's heavy industry, Britain drew

ABOVE: Groundcrew play with a ball next to an 85 Squadron Hurricane at Lille-Seclin at the height of the Phoney War in November 1939.

up plans to invade Norway from where they could intercept Swedish cargo ships. However, Hitler struck first and on April 9, German forces invaded Denmark and Norway.

The Royal Navy was the first to intervene, followed by the landing of British troops, as well as some French units. For the first time, British soldiers were engaged in full-scale combat with the Germans with, in total, more than 50,000 troops being deployed. The Germans, though, had twice that number. The Allies were forced to evacuate some of their troops, though fighting continued into the first week of May.

The Norway campaign was seen as a complete fiasco. By the beginning of May, the situation, both politically and militarily, at home and on the continent, was moving fast, and the government, and in particular the Prime Minister, came under increasing pressure. As Chamberlain was about to discover to his cost, the days ahead were to be full of drama.

NOTES

1. Max Arthur, *Forgotten Voices of the Second World War* (Edbury Press, London, 2005), p.7.
2. Constantine Fitzgibbon, *The Blitz* (Wingate, London, 1957), p.26.
3. Quoted in Angus Cader, *The People's War, Britain 1939-1945* (Panther, London, 1969), p.58.
4. *The Times*, September 5, 1939.
5. *The Times*, August 25, 1939.
6. House of Commons Debate, June 5, 1939; *Hansard*, vol 348 cc17-8.
7. E.S. Turner, *The Phoney War on the Home Front* (Quality Book Club, London, 1961), p.131.
8. ibid.

'Blood, toil, sweat and tears'

The war was not going well, and the country was becoming increasingly dissatisfied with the performance of the Government. There was clamour for change, few, though, could have anticipated just how much would change in the course of just four days in May 1940.

The House of Commons was packed, and those Members of Parliament who had arrived late were standing wherever they could find space. At 15.48 hours on Tuesday, May 7, 1940, Neville Chamberlain, Prime Minister and Leader of the Conservative Party, rose to deliver the opening words of what was to be the most momentous debate in the Mother of Parliaments since the days of Oliver Cromwell.

The subject of the debate was the conduct of the war which had been prompted by an adjournment motion concerning the progress of the campaign in Norway. Such a motion allowed MPs to speak freely without fear of a lashing from the Chief Whip, and there was much for Members to discuss. The operations in Norway were proving humiliatingly disastrous, and Chamberlain was compelled to accept his handling of the war had not been a resounding success. "We have suffered a certain loss of prestige," he conceded, "that a certain colour has been given to the false legend of German invincibility on land, that some discouragement has been caused to our friends, and that our enemies are crowing".[1] »

BELOW: On April 8, 1940, the destroyer HMS *Glowworm* encountered a German force heading for Norway with troops intended for the imminent invasion, Operation *Weserübung*. In the ensuing battle, *Glowworm* was badly damaged by the heavy cruiser *Admiral Hipper*. This picture, taken from the latter, shows the destroyer under fire and making smoke – note the shell splash near *Glowworm*'s stern. (USNHHC)

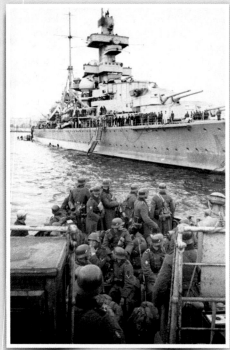

ABOVE: Following its encounter with HMS *Glowworm*, *Admiral Hipper* resumed its original mission, and is subsequently seen here landing troops in Norway. (Bundesarchiv; Bild 101I-757-0038N-11A)

ABOVE: The invasion of Norway underway in 1940 – German troops resting during a break in their march to Northern Norway. (USNHHC)

Nevertheless, the Prime Minister remained defiant: "The campaign is not yet finished. A large part of Norway is not in German hands. The King and the Government are still on Norwegian soil, and they will rally round them the remainder of the Norwegian forces to carry on the fight against the invader."

MPs were amazed with Chamberlain's apparent denial in the face of the facts, with derisive laughter and disbelieving calls from the back benches. The campaign was proving a disaster, with British troops in southern Norway being forced to evacuate.

BELOW: Another view of HMS *Glowworm* during the engagement with *Admiral Hipper*. In the chaos of battle, *Glowworm* rammed the heavy cruiser, a move which sealed her fate. She sank along with 109 of her crew, including her captain, Lieutenant Commander Gerard Roope. For his actions, Roope was posthumously awarded the Victoria Cross. (via Historic Military Press)

It was true that the campaign was still ongoing, but the result was already obvious and the question that Sir Archibald Sinclair, the MP for Caithness and Sutherland and Leader of the Liberal Party, demanded an answer to why the Government had involved the country in an operation that would inevitably lead to defeat: "There were a great many other Members besides myself who foresaw that the German counterstroke, which Ministers had watched in preparation, was likely to be launched with lightning swiftness and ruthless energy the moment the Germans got wind of what we were doing."

To this, back benchers shouted, "They missed the bus!". Clement Atlee, Leader of the Labour Party, pounced on this, agreeing that: "Norway follows Czechoslovakia and Poland. Everywhere the story is 'too late'."

Brigadier-General Sir Henry Croft, the Member of Parliament for Bournemouth, tried to ease the mounting hostility to the Prime Minister by expressing his wish that in the situation the country was in, there would be "an absolute elimination of all old party divisions". It was not to be. The Opposition smelt blood, with Atlee calling for a change of Government: "I say that there is a widespread feeling in this country, not that we shall lose the war, that we will win the war, but that to win the war, we want different people at the helm from those who have led us into it." The knives were out for Neville Chamberlain.

"To win the war, we want different people at the helm from those who have led us into it."

ABOVE: German horse-drawn supply wagons and heavy field guns parked in a Norwegian town, during the march northwards as part of Operation *Weserübung*. (USNHHC)

At 23.00 hours, the House divided. The Government had a working majority of more than 200, but many Conservative members either voted with the Opposition or abstained. Chamberlain survived the vote, but with a majority of just eighty-one. Still failing to see the writing on the wall, for the next two days, Chamberlain tried to form a coalition government with the other parties, only to be told by the Opposition leaders that they would participate in a coalition but not under his leadership. The country needed a new Prime Minister.

THE NATIONAL COALITION
In the midst of this political turmoil, the following morning, Friday, May 10, came stunning news from the Continent – the Germans had invaded the Low Countries. The so-called Phoney War had come to a crashing conclusion. »

"IN THE NAME OF GOD, GO!"
As the day progressed the Commons slowly emptied, and there were barely a dozen members present when Leo Amery, Member for Birmingham Sparkbrook, and himself a Conservative, attracted the Speaker's attention a little after 20.00 hours. "Somehow or other we must get into the Government men who can match our enemies in fighting spirit, in daring, in resolution and in thirst for victory," Amery declared. "We are fighting to-day for our life, for our liberty, for our all; we cannot go on being led as we are."

Pointing at Chamberlain and in little more than a whisper in a hushed Chamber, Amery uttered the words spoken by Cromwell 300 years earlier to the Long Parliament: "You have sat too long here for any good you have been doing. Depart, I say, and let us have done with you. In the name of God, go."

Following this, when MPs sat the next day, Labour's Herbert Morrison called for the adjournment motion to be scrapped and instead demanded a vote of "censure" on Chamberlain's handling of the war. Chamberlain, failing to gauge the degree of opposition to his leadership, delivered a bullish reply: "No Government can prosecute a war efficiently unless it has public and Parliamentary support. I accept the challenge. I welcome it indeed. At least we shall see who is with us and who is against us."

In the heated debate that followed, Winston Churchill, First Lord of the Admiralty, stood up and spoke frankly: "I take complete responsibility for everything that has been done by the Admiralty, and I take my full share of the burden." To this, Lloyd George, in his last major parliamentary contribution, said: "The right honourable Gentleman must not allow himself to be converted into an air-raid shelter to keep the splinters from hitting his colleagues." It would be Churchill who would take on the burden not only of sheltering his colleagues, but of defending the entire nation.

ABOVE: Wherever the Germans unleashed the Blitzkrieg, destruction rained from the air. This is the town of Voss in western Norway burning after a Luftwaffe attack. (Courtesy of Harald Ødegaard)

ABOVE: Rombaksfjord, near Narvik, was the scene of a naval engagement, the First Naval Battle of Narvik, between German destroyers and British naval units on April 10, 1940. This view of the fjord was taken by a German cameraman circa 1942. (USNHHC)

BELOW: Wrecked German destroyers in Rombaksfjord after the naval engagement there on April 10, 1940. (USNHHC)

ABOVE: Another Royal Navy casualty of the Battle of Norway. Here the destroyer HMS *Kelly* is pictured after being torpedoed amidships by the German E-boat S 31 on the night of May 9, 1940. This picture was taken by a Lockheed Hudson of Coastal Command's 224 Squadron on May 10, 1940, whilst the aircraft was acting as escort during the destroyer's return to Newcastle. (Historic Military Press)

"I am not now going to make any comment upon the debates in the House of Commons which took place on Tuesday and Wednesday last. But when it was over, I had no doubt in my mind, that some new and drastic action must be taken if confidence was to be restored the House of Commons, and the war carried on with the vigour and energy which are essential to victory.

"What was that action to be? It was clear, that at this critical moment in the war, what was needed was the formation of a government which included members of the Labour and Liberal oppositions, and thus present a united front to the enemy… By the afternoon of today, it was apparent that the essential unity could be secured under another Prime Minister, though not under myself. In those circumstances my duty was plain. I sought an audience of the King this evening and tended to him my resignation… The King has now entrusted to my friend and colleague, Mr Winston Churchill, the task of forming a new administration on a national basis."

Chamberlain had already accepted that he had to stand down, coming to an agreement with the Labour Party the previous day that he would resign in favour of Churchill, one of the very few politicians untainted with the smear of appeasement. But in light of the German attack, Chamberlain was worried that a change of government at such a time might be highly dangerous. But Atlee was insistent. He would not serve under Chamberlain.

At 21.00 hours that evening Chamberlain spoke to the nation on the BBC: "Early this morning, without room or excuse, Hitler added another to the horrible crimes which already disgrace his name by a sudden attack on Holland, Luxemburg and Belgium. In all history no other man has been responsible for such a hideous total of human suffering and misery as he.

"He has chosen a moment when perhaps it seemed to him that this country was entangled in the throes of a political crisis and when he might find it divided against itself. If he has counted on our internal divisions to help him, he has miscalculated the mind of this people."

ABOVE: A German paratrooper gathers in his parachute having landed in the Netherlands on May 10, 1940. (Dutch National Archives)

BELOW: Another picture of HMS *Kelly* after being torpedoed on the night of May 9, 1940. Despite appearances, the severely damaged *destroyer* was taken under tow. She was repaired and returned to service. (Historic Military Press)

Characteristically, Churchill set about that task with relish. Agreement between himself and the other Party leaders was quickly achieved. He wisely asked Chamberlain to continue as Leader of the Conservative Party as well as offering him Leadership of the House of Commons as well as the Lord Presidency, both of which were accepted. Churchill was far from popular in the Commons and the Conservatives had a very healthy majority. Keeping Chamberlain onboard ensured that the new Coalition Cabinet would have sufficient support from MPs to pass any legislation that might be required.

Wishing to avoid as much disruption as possible during the transition to the new administration, Churchill sent a message to Chamberlain on the morning of May 11, in which he told the former Prime Minister that: "No one changes houses for a month." So, Chamberlain remained in Downing Street while Churchill continued to live at Admiralty House where he made its Map Room his temporary headquarters.

Churchill wanted to keep the War Cabinet, which would oversee the direction of the war, as small as possible, comprising just six members. He created for himself the new post of Minister of Defence, with "undefined" powers, being careful, in his own words, "not to define my rights and duties", but in which he ascribed to himself the supervision of the Chiefs of Staff Committee. As he pointed out, being also Prime Minister, he had, "very wide powers of selection and removal of all professional and political personages".[2] Churchill was in charge of the war effort with almost unlimited authority – and on that day, May 11, the course of the war on the Continent appeared to be going more or less to plan.

BLITZKRIEG

Though the men of the British Expeditionary Force had spent the months since their arrival on the Franco-Belgian border constructing more than forty miles of field fortifications, as soon as word was received that the Germans had invaded Belgium, those positions were abandoned and the troops were moved up to a new position on the River Dyle. They were supported by the French 1st and 7th armies on either flank. If this line could be held, it would mean that a large part of Belgium would be saved from invasion and its main industrial areas would be preserved.

The British and French troops braced themselves for the German onslaught, little knowing that they had been drawn into a trap. On the 13th, the first skirmishes took place along the British sector, though there was no engagement of any consequence. But some seventy miles to the south of the forward British and French positions there were reports that German forces, having marched through the Ardennes, had crossed the Belgian River Meuse.

At this early stage in the unfolding battle, the true consequences of this approach by the Germans was not fully appreciated. The French high command considered the densely-wooded and hilly terrain of the Ardennes to be effectively impenetrable to a modern army with all its motorised encumbrances and the line of the River Meuse easily defendable against light forces. This misconception resulted in the border along the Ardennes having received comparatively little attention and only a small number of pillboxes and bunkers had been built. As a result, when Generalmajor Erwin Rommel's 7th Panzer Division massed on the banks of the Meuse, the French had no means of stopping the German armour.

With the BEF and the French First Army holding off the German attacks and the French Second and Third armies manning the Maginot Line and associated areas, now that the panzers were across the Meuse there was little to stop them racing unimpeded across northern France. At a single stroke, all of France's defensive plans were thrown into chaos. Just days after the start of the fighting, it appeared that Hitler was on the verge of an astonishing victory, and the British and French armies on the brink of disaster. It was time for the Prime Minister to address the country, but first it was to Parliament that Churchill spoke.

"FORWARD TOGETHER"

The House of Commons sat on May 13 for the first time since the end of the Norway debate four days earlier. While telling MPs that he would only give a short summary of events, it would prove to be one of the most memorable and most frequently quoted (often inaccurately) speeches ever delivered in Parliament: "We are in the preliminary stage of one of the greatest battles in history," he told his fellow politicians, "that we are in action at many other points in Norway and in Holland, that we have to be prepared in the Mediterranean".

Churchill also made it clear, possibly in reference to the raising of a volunteer defence force, something that Churchill ➤➤

ABOVE: Having jumped from a trio of Junkers Ju 52s, German Fallschirmjäger, parachute troops, land to the east of The Hague in the Netherlands early on the morning of May 10, 1940. This scene was photographed from the home of H. Lamme, the then chairman of the Dutch Association of Photojournalists, who lived at Helenastraat 2 in The Hague.
(Dutch National Archives)

ABOVE: Enemy forces crossing the border into Luxembourg as part of *Fall Gelb*, the codename for the German invasion of the Low Countries, on May 10, 1940. The attack on this small nation began at 04.35 hours that morning; facing only light resistance, Luxembourg was occupied within a single day. Its government escaped to London, where a government-in-exile was formed.

The need for some form of Home defence had become apparent almost as soon as Hitler had launched his attack upon the Low Countries. An urgent message was issued by the Air Ministry at midday on May 10 to all its Commands which was repeated to the Admiralty, the War Office and the Ministry of Home Security: "Information from Norway shews [*sic*] that German parachute troops, when descending, hold their arms above their heads as if surrendering. The parachutist, however, holds a grenade in each hand. These are thrown at anyone attempting to obstruct the landing. To counter this strategy, parachutists, if they exceed six in number, are to be treated as hostile and if possible shot in the air."

That same day, the *News of the World* printed the following statement by "an ex-serviceman" on its front page: "Germans are dropping by parachute. They may do the same in this country. I am speaking for thousands if not millions of ex-Servicemen who can shoot. We are too old for active service but can show a rifle and a badge and 'let 'em all come'."

had suggested at the beginning of the war, that preparations also "have to be made here at home". Indeed, it was as early as October 8, 1939, that the ever-combative Churchill had written to the Lord Privy Seal, Samuel Hoare, proposing the creation of a 'Home Guard' force of some 500,000 men.

Returning to the House of Commons on May 13, it was the following sentence spoken by Churchill, one of the most famous that he ever made, which captured the spirit of the struggle to come: "I would say to the House, as I said to those who have joined this Government – 'I have nothing to offer but blood, toil, tears and sweat'."

A master orator, the new Prime Minister paused to allow the gravity of his words to sink in. He was, despite his words, able to offer the House something – hope: "We have before us an ordeal of the most grievous kind. We have before us many, many long months of struggle and of suffering. You ask, what is our policy? I will say: It is to wage

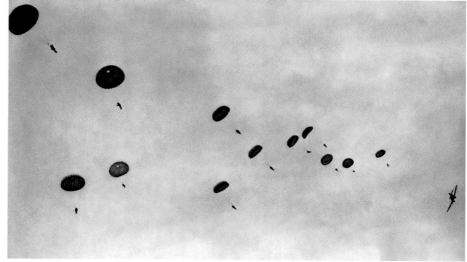

ABOVE: German Fallschirmjäger pictured during the attack on Fort Eben-Emael on 10 May 1940. This Belgian fortress occupied a strategic position that dominated several important bridges over the Albert Canal. The fact that these men are not glider-borne would indicate that they were amongst the reinforcement dropped by a number of Junkers Ju 52 transports as the attack on the Belgian fortress continued.

war, by sea, land and air, with all our might and with all the strength that God can give us; to wage war against a monstrous tyranny never surpassed in the dark, lamentable catalogue of human crime. That is our policy.

"You ask, what is our aim? I can answer in one word: It is victory, victory at all costs, victory in spite of all terror, victory, however long and hard the road may be; for without victory, there is no survival. Let that be realised; no survival for the British Empire, no survival for all that the British Empire has stood for, no survival for the urge and impulse of the ages, that mankind will move forward towards its goal. But I take up my task with buoyancy and hope. I feel sure that our cause will not be suffered to fail among men. At this time, I feel entitled to claim the aid of all, and I say, 'Come then, let us go forward together with our united strength'."[3]

Also, on May 10, a group of businessmen meeting in Leeds decided to take matters into their own hands. "It was unanimously agreed," recalled one of those present, a Captain Mason, "that such a menace to England might be met if ex-Servicemen were given fire-arms. We all felt that here was a job for the men of the last war." It was Mason who also suggested a name for this new force – L.A.D.S., or the Local Auxiliary Defence Service.[4]

The significance of the news from the Continent was the information received that the Germans had made effective use of parachutists in their invasion of Belgium and the Netherlands. If parachutists could be dropped into Holland, they could just as easily be dropped on Great Britain. With its soldiers fighting for their lives on the

ABOVE: A German self-propelled gun on the move through Cambrai during the invasion of France and the Low Countries in 1940. According to the original annotation that accompanied the image, the unit is Panzerjäger SFL Pz.Jg. I. Note the abandoned British Army lorries in the background. (Historic Military Press)

ABOVE: Pictured by a German soldier during the Blitzkrieg in 1940, this French road is lined by refugees who had attempted to flee from the advancing enemy troops. (Historic Military Press)

ABOVE: As the Blitzkrieg rolls relentlessly westwards, German troops are pictured advancing through dusty French roads in May or June 1940. (Historic Military Press)

British troops being marched off into captivity in Cambrai, May 1940. (Historic Military Press)

Continent, there was no armed force in the UK to deal with such a threat.

The next day, May 11, a meeting was held in which General Sir John Dill, Vice Chief of the Imperial General Staff, General Sir Robert Gordon-Finlayson, the Adjutant General, and General Sir Walter Kirke, Inspector-General of Home Defence, met with Oliver Stanley, whose last day it was as Secretary of State for War, though he was unaware of this at the time. The subject of the meeting was Home Defence and the possible measures that could be taken to combat the threat of German parachutists landing in Britain.

As the one most responsible for homeland defence, General Kirke stated that he had, for some time, been considering the possibility of directing the "rising tide of martial enthusiasm" around the country into an organised body of some description which could be fitted into the existing defence structures and commands. Kirke believed that volunteers should be organised and financed on a decentralised basis and kept as simple as possible.

Time was a major factor in his thinking. With the threat of aerial assaults potentially imminent, there would not be time to build a complex organisation. The situation being considered extremely serious, a very prompt decision needed to be made. Consequently, Kirke's suggestion was accepted in principle, the general being asked to sketch out firm proposals in readiness for a second meeting in two days' time.

What Kirke proposed at the War Office on the 13th was for the formation of a defence force established on a town and village basis, giving the most possible latitude to local initiatives so that the scheme could be enacted in the shortest possible time. Kirke would almost certainly been aware that people were already ahead of the government.

Whilst the authorities had prevaricated, across the nation there were individuals like Captain Mason whose desire to take action was so strong that they had already formed themselves into ad hoc units to deal with enemy parachutists. One afternoon in March 1940, for example, Lady Helena Gleichen, a grand-niece of Queen Victoria, walked into the headquarters of a battalion of the King's Shropshire Light Infantry based at Ross-on-Wye. Lady Gleichen promptly announced that she had become so alarmed at the

threat of German parachute troops landing in the area around her ancestral home in Herefordshire that she had formed her own defence force – the Much Marcle Watchers. The volunteers were recruited from the staff at Lady Gleichen's large stately home or the tenants on the estate, and patrols from the eighty or so members were on duty every night, each individual wearing an armband with "Much Marcle Watchers" stencilled on it. Weapons though, were a major concern for Lady Gleichen and it was for this reason that she had called on the KSLI and asked for the loan of eighty rifles, some ammunition and "a couple of machine guns if you have any".

To the government, it was only a short step to bring such groups under more regulated control. While there were still many factors to be taken into account, agreement was reached – it was time to start recruiting what was to be called the Local Defence Volunteers.

NOTES

1. See *Hansard*, House of Commons Debates, vol. 360, May 7-9, 1940.
2. Winston S. Churchill, *The Second World War, Volume II, Their Finest Hour* (Cassell, London, 1949), pp.3-24.
3. *Hansard*, May 13, 1940.
4. Charles Graves, *The Home Guard of Britain* (Hutchinson & Co., London, 1943), p.177.

BELOW: A horse-drawn German column pictured on the approaches to the Ferme de Navarin War Memorial during the Blitzkrieg in the summer of 1940. Situated twenty-eight miles east of Reims, the imposing Ferme de Navarin War Memorial is a combined monument and ossuary, within which lie the remains of 10,000 soldiers who fell on the plains of Champagne in the First World War. (Historic Military Press)

"We all felt that here was a job for the men of the last war."

A Proud Tradition

That many inside and outside the government had been considering the question of a volunteer army was perhaps unsurprising, for Britain had a long history of its citizens taking up arms for the nation's defence.

BELOW: Men of "D" Company, 12th Battalion Surrey Volunteer Training Corps on parade. (Historic Military Press)

The concept of nationally arranged, though locally organised, defensive forces in England can be traced back at least as far as the 9th century, when Alfred the Great developed a network of fortified settlements (known as burhs) with interconnecting roads to counter the persistent incursions of the dreaded Vikings. Each burh had an armed defence force, possibly mounted, which would assemble when the Vikings appeared. The prime purpose of the burghal force, the fyrd, was to provide defence for a port or town, and the surrounding farms, villages and hamlets. It was Alfred's intention that no English farm or village would be more than 20 miles away from a burh. In addition to the local fyrd, there was a royal fyrd, which was a body of professional warriors that served directly under the king. This system equated to the regular army and the territorials, and, of course, the LDV and Home Guard, of more recent times.

With the passage of time, the requirements of the country, and the obligations imposed upon its citizenry to undertake military service, varied with the needs of whichever monarch was incumbent at the time. It was not until 1285 that the militia system was established in law with Edward I's Statue of Windsor, whereby every male between the ages of 16 and 60 was, theoretically, required to serve in the militia, albeit only for a certain number of days each year. This item of legislation formulated the Commissions of Array which became the standard method of raising a field army from the shire levies.

This act was repealed in 1558, being replaced by the Militia Act, in which each individual's military obligations were re-defined based on their financial status. Thus a man worth only £5 to £10 a year was expected to provide just a coat of plated armour, a pike or halberd, a longbow and a helmet, whereas those worth £1,000 or more were obliged to supply 16 horses, 80 suits of light armour, 40 pikes, 30 bows, 20 bills or halberds, 20 arquebuses and 50 helmets.[1]

This, though, was swept away in the English Civil War with the introduction of a small, professional, standing army, which was supplemented by locally raised militias under the control of county lord lieutenants. It was the duty of Justices of the Peace to ensure that the parish constables in their respective districts mustered the militia when required.

When the Kingdom of Great Britain was formed in 1707, separate militia were established for both Scotland, and England and Wales. This changed again in 1801, when Ireland joined what became the United Kingdom of Great Briton and Ireland, the force becoming the Militia of the United Kingdom. The threat at that time came from Napoleon Bonaparte's France, prompting an array of volunteer local militias. »

BELOW: Mirroring scenes barely twenty years later, a Volunteer Training Corps, or VTC, unit is pictured parading on "Empire Day" during the First World War, though the exact year is not known. The original caption indicates that this is a Bristol-based VTC unit.
(Historic Military Press)

"On the Continent, the Germans had made significant gains, almost reaching Paris and invasions fears began to mount."

Much as in the two world wars, during Napoleonic times military uniforms were worn with great pride by anyone who could possibly justify it, and many private regiments were raised by wealthy individuals (with Army approval) which enabled those individuals to obtain the prestigious rank of colonel. Large scale field days began during this time, with thousands of volunteers parading and engaging in mock battles to the delight of very large admiring crowds.

THE VICTORIAN VOLUNTEERS

The Duke of Wellington's successes in the Peninsular War and at Waterloo raised the British Army's standing to unprecedented levels, and there was a huge surge of men wishing to acquire some of that reflected glory. This saw the creation of a large Volunteer Force comprised of small bands of local men consisting of approximately 100 all ranks under the command of a captain, with some localities having subdivisions of thirty men under a lieutenant. The purpose of the rifle volunteers was to harass the invading enemy's flanks, while artillery volunteers were to man coastal guns and forts – very much as the Home Guard would be expected to do 100 years later.

The last major re-structuring of Britain's part-time forces came in April 1908, with the formation of a new voluntary body, the Territorial Army. The distinctions between the regulars and the part-timers were swept away with the Territorials being, in effect, the reserve force of the British Army, their title later becoming the Territorial Army Volunteer Reserve.

ABOVE: A Volunteer Training Corps officer pictured firing a revolver during training.

There had been a surge in civilian volunteering during the Boer War, but with no possible threat of invasion, local defence was not a consideration. That was far from being the case, however, in 1914.

The outbreak of the Great War saw an enormous rush to Army recruiting offices. This was encouraged by the government which believed that the best way for civilians to contribute to the defence of the country was for them to join the regular forces. But around the UK men were already taking matters into their own hands. As early as

August 6, 1914, just two days after the declaration of war, a member of the London County Council, Percy Harris, had written to *The Times* proposing the formation of a "London volunteer defence force".

Another two days after this proposal had been put forward, both H.G. Wells and Sir Arthur Conan Doyle declared their support for the raising of volunteer defence groups. In fact, volunteers were already being drilled at Windlesham in Sussex. Others began to form local associations and in less than two weeks "town guards" had appeared in Oxfordshire, Buckinghamshire, Lancashire and Surrey.

The government was very uneasy at the prospect of unregulated armed bands at large around the country, especially as it wanted men to be joining the regular Army, plus there was also a shortage of weapons for the recruits in Army training camps. But on the Continent, the Germans had made significant gains, almost reaching Paris and invasion fears began to mount. This led to increasing pressure upon the government to support local defence schemes. Finally, on November 19, 1914, Lord Kitchener, the Secretary of State for War, announced the creation of the Volunteer Training Corps (VTC).

Those wishing to join the new corps had to be men not of military age, unless they had "genuine" reasons for not enlisting in the Army. Volunteers were to receive no government funding and were not permitted to wear any military clothing other than an arm band. This last restriction was quickly rescinded, and volunteers were permitted to wear a green uniform. With this, further impositions were laid down. A series of ranks were established from the lowest rank of "volunteer" to "county commandant". Volunteers were expected to attend forty drills each of an hour's duration and those not attending at least twelve drills in six months would be obliged to resign.[2]

THE 1916 VOLUNTEER ACT

Gradually, the VTC received greater government recognition and in July 1916, the training corps became "volunteer regiments" and, as such, came under the 1863 Volunteer Act. This meant enforceable discipline could be imposed, which took the form of fines which were recoverable through the civil courts. Officers could also receive recognised commissions. The only problem with the 1863 Act was that anyone enlisted as a volunteer was exempt from military duty and with the introduction of conscription there was obviously going to be many who would try to avoid being sent to the trenches by joining a volunteer regiment. A new piece of legislation was brought in to help solve this – the 1916 Volunteer Act – which required volunteers to serve for the duration of hostilities, to participate in a statutory minimum of fourteen, later reduced to ten, drills per month and, more significantly, to undertake limited military duties as required.

The new act introduced distinct categories of volunteer eligibility, two of which were regarding those who were too young or too old for military service. Those who were of military age, had to be unfit for any other

ABOVE: Following the organisation's formation, authority for its members to carry out their duties was often displayed by the wearing of a red arm band with the letters "G R" in gold – such as seen here on this VTC volunteer. (Historic Military Press)

form of service or be in key jobs, such as special constables and railway workers, who might not be available in an emergency.

There was, from January 1917, a War Office grant of £2 per annum for those too old (over the age of 41) or too young (under the age of 18) to join the armed forces for the purchase of equipment and other costs.

In theory, this sum was supposed to cover all expenses, but this was rarely the case and volunteers still had to dig into their own pockets or raise funds locally.

The volunteer regiments were regarded as being of little fighting value. They were also, generally, poorly armed. As late as the summer of 1917, the 1st Fife Volunteer Battalion, for example, had only 130 rifles for its 1,900 men, and the 1st City of Aberdeen Battalion 190 rifles to share between 1,007 volunteers.[3] Morale, which was high at first when the volunteers were men who genuinely wanted to join a military force to help defend the country, gradually decreased as the war progressed. This, it was said, was because of a large number of men who had sought to avoid conscription by appealing to the Military Service Tribunals, had been pressed into the ranks of the volunteer regiments. By late 1918, when conscription had been extended to include men up to the age of 50, such "tribunal" men made up 44 per cent of the volunteer battalions.

Such issues aside, at its peak the VTC had nearly 300,000 members. Whilst the Corps was disbanded at the end of the war, many valuable lessons had been learnt that would prove useful to some just over twenty years later.

NOTES

1. L. Boynton, *The Elizabethan Militia 1558-1638* (Routledge and Kegan Paul, London, 1967), p.9.
2. Ian F.W. Beckett, *Britain's Part-Time Soldiers, The Amateur Military Tradition 1558-1945* (Pen & Sword, Barnsley, 2011), pp.237-8.
3. ibid, p.240.

ABOVE: Members of a seemingly well-armed VTC unit in the Clapham Junction area pose for a group photograph. (Historic Military Press)

The Local Defence Volunteers

The call went out for volunteers to defend the nation, and the men responded – not just in their tens of thousands as had been expected, but in their hundreds of thousands.

It had been Oliver Stanley's intention to broadcast an appeal for volunteers on May 11, but as so many details had to be considered before such a measure could be undertaken, the announcement was delayed. It was then thought that the broadcast should be given by the Commander-in-Chief Home Forces. However, when Anthony Eden took over Stanley's position of Secretary of State for War, it was considered more appropriate that he, as an elected politician, should be the one to make the announcement.

In the House of Commons on May 13, 1940, James Henderson-Stewart, the MP for Fife Eastern, questioned the new Secretary of State for War as to "whether, in order to meet the imminent danger of enemy parachute landings in this country and avoid displacing regular troops, he will consider the immediate formation of a voluntary corps composed of older, responsible men to be armed with rifles and Bren guns and trained for instant action in their own localities, in case of raids?" In reply, Eden confirmed that "this matter has been receiving urgent attention in the light of recent events, and I hope to make an announcement on the subject at a very early date".[1]

In fact, Eden's speech, his first as Secretary of State for War, came a little more than 24 hours later. His words had been penned late on the evening of May 13 in conjunction with General Kirke, who, in turn, had referred to a series of notes made by General Gordon-Finlayson.

A NATIONAL APPEAL

The Blitzkrieg unleashed by Hitler's forces in France and the Low Countries was barely four days old, and having been made aware that an important speech was to be given, an expectant nation gathered around its radio sets to hear what the new Secretary of State for War had to say. Shortly after nine o'clock on the evening of May 14, Eden's voice crackled out across the airwaves via the BBC's Home Service:

"I want to speak to you to-night about the form of warfare which the Germans have been employing so extensively against Holland and Belgium – namely, the dropping of troops by parachute behind the main defensive lines… Their function is to seize important points, such as aerodromes, power stations, villages, railway junctions and telephone exchanges, either for the purpose of destroying them at once, or of holding them until the arrival of reinforcements. The purpose of the parachute attack is to disorganise and confuse, as a preparation for the landing of troops by aircraft. »

MAIN PICTURE: With a very real threat of invasion hanging over the country, barricades sprang up throughout the UK – such as this example pictured on May 27, 1940. Roadblocks like these were soon being manned by the men of the fledgling LDV.
(Historic Military Press)

ABOVE: A portrait of Antony Eden, whose broadcast on the evening of May 14, 1940 generated a remarkable response throughout Britain.
(Library of Congress)

"I rushed to the police station immediately the broadcast had finished."

ABOVE: A unit of the Local Defence Volunteers on parade soon after their formation in the summer of 1940. Note the mix of civilian and military clothing, as well as the medal ribbons worn by some of the men. (Historic Military Press)

BELOW: A newspaper cutting which shows members of the LDV enrolling in May 1940. (Historic Military Press)

LOCAL DEFENCE VOLUNTEERS
Thousands of men between the ages of 17 and 65 registered at their local police stations for service with the Local Defence Volunteers, Britain's new anti-parachute army. Here is a typical scene as a group of volunteers were being enrolled at Sevenoaks.

"The success of such an attack depends on speed. Consequently, the measures to defeat such an attack must be prompt and rapid. It is upon this basis that… we are going to ask you to help us, in a manner which I know will be welcome to thousands of you. Since the war began the Government have received countless enquiries from all over the Kingdom from men of all ages who are for one reason or another not at present engaged in military service, and who wish to do something for the defence of the country.

"Now is your opportunity. We want large numbers of such men in Great Britain who are British subjects, between the ages of 17 and 65, to come forward now and offer their service in order to make assurance doubly sure. The name of the new force which is now to be raised will be the 'Local Defence

Volunteers'. This name, Local Defence Volunteers, describes its duties in three words. It must be understood that this is, so to speak, a spare-time job, so there will be no need for any volunteer to abandon his present occupation."

KEEPING THE COUNTRY SAFE

Eden then explained that part-time members of existing civil defence organisations should ask their commanders' advice before registering under the scheme, whilst men who would eventually be called up for National Service would be permitted to join on a temporary basis until required to enlist in the regular armed forces. The Secretary of State said that when on duty, volunteers would form part of the country's military and that they would be obliged to serve for the duration of the war. Volunteers would not be paid but would receive a uniform. Optimistically, he confirmed that they would all be armed and trained to use such weapons.

Volunteers were told to give their names at their local police station and that they would be contacted as and when required. "This appeal is directed chiefly to those who live in small towns, villages and less densely inhabited suburban areas," Eden concluded. "I must warn you that, for certain military

reasons, there will be some localities where the numbers required will be small, and others where your services will not be required at all. Here then is the opportunity for which so many of you have been waiting. Your loyal help, added to the arrangements which already exist, will make and keep our country safe."

POLICE STATIONS UNDER SIEGE

The response to Eden's appeal was both immediate and dramatic. In some cases, the broadcast had not even ended before Police stations found themselves swamped with men eager to enlist. "I rushed to the police station immediately the broadcast had finished," one Surbiton man told a reporter, "but I found a long queue had arrived there before me".

ABOVE: A group of early Local Defence Volunteers in Cheshire prepare to go out on patrol as 'para-spotters' in May 1940. Note the lack of weapons and the improvised arm bands. (Historic Military Press)

"No sooner had Mr. Eden finished his talk than police stations in London were inundated with offers of assistance," noted an editorial in *The Times* the following day. "Telephone calls were almost continuous, and hundreds of men visited the police stations to register their names. There were early indications from all over Great Britain of a big response to the appeal. 'Our first recruit walked in four minutes after the broadcast,' was the report at Newcastle city police headquarters. He was the first of a steady stream. The West Riding police headquarters at Wakefield were kept busy answering

ABOVE: An officially produced armband for the Local Defence Volunteers. (Historic Military Press)

ABOVE: An early Local Defence Volunteer on duty on Werneth Low, Cheshire, in May 1940. Note the lack of weapons and the improvised arm band. (Historic Military Press)

telephone inquiries and taking down names. Most of the volunteers were aged 40-50, and 90 per cent. were old soldiers."

The rush continued throughout the 15th, the scenes witnessed at Dover mirroring those seen throughout the county. "Almost immediately men started to arrive at Dover police station," wrote a local historian, "but were told to come back at 08.00hrs the following morning. Over twenty volunteers were at the police station before 08.00hrs, where a specially manned table had been set up. Within an hour, a second table was set up and the call went out for more staff to come in and help out. Throughout the day men, mainly between the ages of 40 and 50 years, signed up, the majority being World War I veterans. They included a General and several musketry instructors."[2] Within the first twenty-four hours some 600 men had enrolled at Dover; nationwide the figure was a staggering 250,000.

It was a similar story in Hampshire. "Within minutes of that appeal going out," noted one reporter, "police stations were besieged by men wishing to sign up. One man arrived at Haslemere police station before Eden had finished speaking and queues quickly formed with men arriving right up until midnight. From 6am the next morning *The Herald* reported men arriving in cars – often with 'private chauffeurs' – to sign up, including one well-known retired solicitor. Professions included retired officers, a dental surgeon, a chemist, an insurance secretary, an engineer, a schoolmaster, a forester, gardeners, grooms, farm workers, and labourers. At one

point, police officers ran out of forms and there were still plenty of men in the queue come Thursday morning."[3]

One of those veterans who had listened to Eden on the BBC was General Sir Hubert Gough GCB, GCMG, KCVO, who had been at his home in Chelsea when he heard the appeal. "Well," he immediately declared, "I am going to have a chance of practising my profession again, after all". He stood up and began to pace about, impatient that he should have to wait until the following day to register.[4]

"Next morning, Gough," wrote his biographer, Anthony Farrar-Hockley, "discovered from the police that volunteers from his part of London were to register at Chelsea Barracks. He walked down there… growing increasingly uneasy that he might find some acquaintance in charge who would remind him that the age limit was sixty-five and so turn him away. With some relief he discovered that the registration office was empty save for book, table and chair: no one seemed to be concerned with the qualifications of the volunteers. Even so, as a precaution he put down the name 'Hubert Goff' against his address and half-regretted afterwards that he had not entered 'esq' as additional protection

ABOVE: A representation of how a typical LDV member might have looked in May 1940. Wearing the ubiquitous LDV armband (being one of the earliest officially issued examples) and his gasmask, he has armed himself with a Molotov Cocktail. (Historic Military Press)

ABOVE: Among the many thousands of men who flocked to enrol in the LDV after Eden's broadcast was General Hubert Gough, a veteran of Britain's wars stretching back into the Victorian era. Gough is pictured here, on the left, whilst accompanying King Albert I of Belgium on an inspection of the Western Front during the First World War, more specifically May 1917. (Dutch National Archives)

of his identity. He was quite prepared to serve incognito as a private."[5] Unsurprisingly, General Gough's true identity was soon revealed, and he was promptly asked to take command of the LDV in his part of London – despite his impending 70th birthday.

CONTRARY TO THE RULES OF INTERNATIONAL LAW

Eden's broadcast was picked up by the German government. Its reaction to learning of the LDV's formation was given in a radio broadcast on May 16, 1940: "The British Government is committing the worst crime of all. Evidently, it permits open preparation for the formation of murder bands. The preparations which are being made all over England to arm the civilian population for guerrilla warfare are contrary to the rules of international law. German official quarters warn the misled British public and remind them the fate of *francs-tireurs* and gangs of murders. Civilians who take up arms against German soldiers are, under international law, no better than murderers, whether they are priests or bank clerks. British people, you will do well to heed our warning."[6] »

RIGHT: A volunteer in the village of West Farleigh, near Maidstone in Kent, tries out his unit's newly-acquired armoured car on August 29, 1940. With cloth caps and much improvisation, ex-Grenadier Guardsman Second Lieutenant J W Oxley, the West Farleigh Platoon Commander, is sat in an old 30hp Buick presented to the unit by a local resident. The transformation to armoured car was achieved by simply welding or bolting steel plating over the windows and radiators. (Historic Military Press)

BELOW: This representation shows how an LDV member might have looked in late June or early July 1940. He has been issued with a later version of the LDV armband, this one with red G.P.O. battalion unit stamps on either side of the 'LDV'. This volunteer is wearing a Universal Pattern Field Service Cap, though unit badges were yet to be authorised. He is armed with a Short Magazine Lee Enfield .303 rifle, more specially a No.1 Mk.3*. Many LDV units were hastily issued with such weapons in the summer of 1940, only for them to be withdrawn at a later stage and replaced with the likes of the P14, P17 or Ross rifles. (Historic Military Press)

But the Germans had completely missed the point. The LDV, and Home Guard as it would become just two months later, was to be armed, given uniforms and fall under the authority, and discipline, of the Army. The LDV would become an official military body, merely on a part-time, unpaid basis.

Undeterred by the enemy's threats, the volunteers continued to step forward. At the same time, many of the embryonic LDV units wasted no time in organising themselves. One volunteer in Northampton, a George Drummond writing on May 17, noted a procedure immediately put in place in his area: "If the [invasion] warning is sounded, two or three cars will at once assemble with the men detailed. Should any parachutists be seen, two cars will at once set off. The leading one to locate the landings and to keep in touch; the other car, when signalled, to go to the nearest telephone and inform the Chief Constable. Any other cars to be similarly used. Men have also been detailed to "mind" the Post Office."[7]

Dick Fulford also recalled the LDV's beginning: "Armed with a 4/10 shotgun and a home-made LDV armband I was detailed to report to a cart shed on the top of one of the Wiltshire Downs. Lord Essex had been appointed C.O. of our village contingent and I, being the youngest, was nominated his 'runner' as telephones were unheard of at that time. The other volunteers were aggressive World War I veterans, all armed with rifles, shot guns, cutlasses and home-made pikes. Look out Hitler, we, the LDV are ready for you!"[8]

As well as weapons, to be "ready" the LDV needed pens, pencils, paper and files to begin the administrative processes as more and more men offered their services, as well as desks and chairs in what were often empty rooms in police stations or village or church halls. As Captain Atkins, of what became the *23rd Warwickshire* (Birmingham) Battalion, described it, this was when the "scrounging" began, with items appearing from nowhere, with no questions being asked concerning their provenance.

Major E.A. Mackay, later Commander of the Trowbridge Company of the Wiltshire

Home Guard, wrote of those first days of the LDV: "Our beginnings were very humble. Headquarters of companies, platoons and even battalions were located in houses or rooms begged or borrowed, in stables, out-houses and parlours… Later, accommodation was requisitioned, and rooms were hired for offices, stores and training. Makeshift also were our look-outs. Shepherds' vans were much in demand and others were made locally with boards and rabbit-netting. Our primitive road-blocks were things to look back at with a shudder. One dreads to think what would have been their fate if they had really been put to the test."[9]

Jack Scarr was another of those who responded to Eden's broadcast. "I promptly cycled to Hemel Hempstead and gave my details," he later recalled. "Our duties were to be the eyes of the Regulars, to patrol the countryside, watching anyone behaving suspiciously near bridges, crossroads or installations… We were warned that the Germans might land wearing British uniforms or in some other form of disguise… Above all, we were to know our area backwards: where the nearest phone was, the nearest doctor, the nearest first aid post, the position of the nearest Regulars. If we were manning a post or road block, we must hold it to the last and delay the enemy as long as possible… On many an evening over those early months the question uppermost in our minds was 'Will they come tonight?'."[10]

"WHO WENT THERE?"

ABOVE: Two cartoons that presents a comical look at the LDV in 1940. To some, the letters LDV soon came to mean 'Look, Duck and Vanish'. (via Historic Military Press)

ABOVE: A card entitled 'Notes for Guidance of LMS Members of the Local Volunteer Defence Corps' which, dated June 1940, was issued to staff of the London, Midland and Scottish Railway who had enlisted in the LDV. (Historic Military Press)

AN EXTRA SECURITY

The challenge for the authorities was just how this new military force, the ranks of which continued to swell with every passing day, was to operate. At 20.57 hours on the evening of May 22, 1940, Sir Edward Grigg rose to speak in the House of Commons to answer questions that many in Parliament, and the country as a whole, were asking on this subject. As well as sitting as the MP for Altrincham, Grigg was the Under-Secretary of State for War who had been asked by Eden to assume control of the LDV's formation, and as such was best placed to explain how it was organised and controlled.

"The House will feel that we owe a great debt of gratitude to the organisers who have undertaken this work and also to the patriotism of the volunteers who have come forward," Grigg announced to a packed House of Commons. "It is a remarkable sign of the readiness of this country to come

forward when it is called upon. We have called upon a hitherto untapped source of defence, and this experience shows what reserves of patriotism we possess."

Confirming some of the information already announced, Grigg then outlined the basics of the LDV's structure – though he was mindful of the need to not reveal too much. The Local Defence Volunteers are, he did note, "based upon the military organisation and is organised by areas like the military commands. Each area has been sub-divided into zones, and each zone is sub-divided into groups, the groups into companies, and the companies into platoons and sections. There is a regular chain of command the whole way down from the area to the section. At the head of each zone and group are voluntary organisers, and they and the officers chosen to raise the sections are, like the volunteers themselves, unpaid. The whole thing is voluntary."[11]

As his speech continued, Grigg described the functions of the LDV. "I should like to make it clear that the volunteers are a reinforcement of existing organisations for home defence. There is already in existence a very considerable organisation for home defence. We not only have many divisions in various stages of training in this country, but we also have our home defence battalions, and we have other trained troops in this country. The Local Defence Volunteers are, therefore, a reinsurance, an extra security, and will, I believe, be invaluable.

"They will be invaluable in particular in two ways. In the first place, they will prevent the dispersal of first-line troops in small packets. The first duty of the Army is to keep its divisions intact, for service here or overseas, as may be required, and they cannot be kept intact if men are dispersed for guard duties all over the country. The second duty of the Army is to press on with the training and the equipment of new troops, and training, or advanced training, at any rate, becomes impossible if formations are broken up for various purposes of local defence. Dispersal for local defence would mean, in fact, the complete immobilisation of trained divisions and would also bring advanced training to a halt.

"The Local Defence Volunteers can, therefore, render absolutely invaluable service, alike to the Army and the country, by co-operating with home defence battalions in freeing the organised divisions of the Army from the need for meeting the immediate needs of local defence.

"They have another function to perform, a very important function, which is described to some extent by the name popularly given to them of 'para-shootists'. They are wanted to deal with small enemy parties landed »

Members of the Local Defence Volunteers on parade July 1, 1940. Note the medals worn by a number of these men. (via Historic Military Press)

"If we were manning a post or road block, we must hold it to the last."

from the air. We have seen what the effect of the landing of small groups by parachute or aircraft has been in other countries, and it is important to organise means of local action against the measures which these small parties landed in various places may take.

"The three main purposes for which the Local Defence Volunteers are wanted are these: First, observation and information. We want the earliest possible information, either from observation posts or from patrols, as to landings. The second purpose is to help, in the very earliest stages, in preventing movement by these enemy parties landed from the air by blocking roads, by denying them access to means of movement, motors and so on, and by seeing that they are hemmed in as completely as possible from the moment they land. Their third purpose is to assist in patrolling and protecting vulnerable spots, of which there is a great number everywhere, particularly in certain parts of the country where the demands for local guard duties are really greater than the present forces can meet."

The War Office, together with the Home Office, concluded that the Army's military districts would administer the new bodies in their respective areas which in turn were divided into zones based on local police districts. The War Office also issued instructions on how the new bodies were to be organised. They would be arranged into sections, platoons and companies. Selecting the company commanders was a somewhat arbitrary affair, each being chosen by the Army's Area Commanders under the auspices of the county Lord Lieutenants, the latter automatically being the President of his respective County Territorial Army Association.

BEYOND EXPECTATIONS

Before these volunteers could be properly marshalled and organised, groups of citizens had already taken up arms of sorts,

RIGHT: Men of the Rustington LDV pictured with some of their unit's transport early in the summer of 1940. The fact that the volunteer on the far left appears to have a Home Guard armband, whilst the cart carries an LDV sign, suggests this image was taken late in July.
(Courtesy of Mrs Mary Taylor)

BELOW: This plaque on the wall of the former Police Station in Farnborough Common, near Orpington in Kent, commemorates the local Home Guard and specifically mentions the fact the many of the men first enrolled in the LDV in this building. (Courtesy of Christopher Hilton; www.geograph.org.uk)

HERE IN MAY 1940 THE
LOCAL DEFENCE VOLUNTEERS
WERE FIRST ENROLLED TO HELP TO MEET THE
THREATENED GERMAN INVASION THEY BECAME THE
52ND KENT BATTALION HOME GUARD
AND ON DECEMBER 3RD 1944 WHEN ALL DANGER
OF INVASION HAD PASSED THE BATTALION
"STOOD DOWN" OUTSIDE THIS BUILDING

ranging from shotguns to cricket bats, and taken to the streets on the lookout for enemy parachutists or, indeed, for anyone behaving suspiciously. The most pressing concern for the government, therefore, was to lay down some form of structure for the LDV and bring the volunteers under disciplined control. Indeed, further clarification of the organisation's roles was given in Training Instruction No.2, which was issued on 6 June 1940: "The Local Defence Volunteers are neither trained nor equipped to offer strong prolonged resistance to highly trained German troops, and they will, therefore, best fulfil their role by observation, by the rapid transmission of information, and by confining the enemy's activities."

By the end of May, the number of volunteers had climbed to between 300,000 and

400,000, and the rate of enlistment showed little sign of levelling off. "Some in the War Office," wrote the Home Guard historian S.P. MacKenzie, "had apparently been anticipating a maximum of about 150,000 recruits, others perhaps 200,000; even Lord Croft, given to exaggeration, thought that at most 500,000 men would come forward". In what was a truly staggering response, by the end of June 1940 a total of 1,456,000 men had registered as volunteers in the LDV. "My expectations,' remarked a rueful Anthony Eden in August that year, "have been far exceeded".[12]

One volunteer who joined the ranks of General Gough's LDV embryonic unit, described only as a middle-aged milkman, later recalled those early, heady days of its formation: "This letter comes telling us to parade at the Chelsea Hospital. 'What's this,' I said to my wife, 'in with the pensioners?' Not a bit. There was this little general [Gough] charming us all like the birds off a tree, getting the whole mob into line so that the lady mayoress could say her piece.

"Next thing I knew was, we were marched off to the local Territorial Army drill hall, all the men I'd been standing with in the parade: we were all made into one company. There weren't any weapons, except a few shotguns kept for sentries. So, the general's orders were [to train in] map-reading, fieldcraft and, as you might expect, drill. Did we like it? We loved it!"[13]

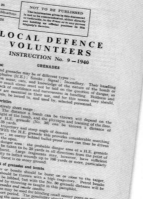

ABOVE: Some of the instructions printed for the Local Defence Volunteers, these three all being published in July 1940. (Courtesy of Richard Hunt)

NOTES

1. *Hansard*, vol 360 cc1497-8.
2. 'Dover's Home Guard', quoted on www.doverhistorian.com.
3. 'Dad's Army? Don't Panic', in *The Farnham Herald*, March 13, 2016.
4. Anthony Farrar-Hockley, *Goughie: The Life of General Sir Hubert Gough* (Hart-Davis, MacGibbon, St Albans, 1975), p.366.
5. ibid, pp.366-7.
6. Charles Graves, *The Home Guard of Britain* (Hutchison, London), p.16.
7. *The Times*, May 17, 1940.
8. Market Harborough Royal British Legion, BBC People's War, Article ID: A4117835.
9. Major E.A. Mackay, *The History of the Wiltshire Home Guard 1940 – 1944* (Lansdown & Sons, Trowbridge, 1946), p.13.
10. From the memoirs of Sergeant Jack Scarr, 9th Battalion, Hertfordshire Home Guard, 1940-42, quoted on the National Army Museum website: www.nam.ac.uk/explore/britain-alone-1940.
11. *Hansard*, vol 361 cc238-76.
12. S.P. MacKenzie, *The Home Guard* (Oxford University Press, Oxford, 1995), p.35.
13. Anthony Farrar-Hockley, pp.368-9.

Broom Handles and Rifles

As the ranks of the Local Defence Volunteers swelled, the question of arming the men became ever more pressing.

It was genuinely believed in those early days of the Local Defence Volunteers, with the Germans overrunning France, that Britain would soon be invaded. Colonel C W Marsden, commanding a sector near Chester, was summoned to a gathering in a large hotel in the city, where the assembled LDV leaders were briefed by an "eminent" politician who explained: "How we were to be invaded at any moment; how we were to fight the Hun with lumps of lead piping and to have home-made bombs – though from whose home they were to emanate or be thrown he didn't say – at the enemy. We would die in thousands, but some of us would remain, and as there was nowhere for us to run we should stay on and fight."[1]

However, despite such chilling predictions, one of the challenges facing organisers was retaining the volunteers' interest, particularly as few weapons were initially available. This shortage also limited the amount of training which could be given to the men. One unit solved this by acquiring eighty dummy rifles from the local Boys' Brigade. Thankfully, most of the initial intake were veterans of the First World War who needed little or no training in the use of firearms.

But without weapons, many of the volunteers started to become disillusioned. The pressure upon the authorities to arm the LDV became an even greater dilemma when the men of the BEF escaped from Dunkirk at the end of May with only the weapons they could carry. The British Army was almost

devoid of heavy weaponry and armoured vehicles, and priority had to be given to re-arming the regular forces before any consideration could be given to the LDV.

An immediate order was placed for a shipment of 75,000 First World War-vintage Ross Rifles from Canada, as well as 100,000 Springfield and Remington rifles from the United States. These, though, would not arrive before July, so Richard Law, Finance Secretary to the War Office, appealed for all persons not already enrolled in the LDV who possessed shotguns and rifles to hand them in at police stations so that they could be distributed to local LDV units. Despite the many years of pre-war efforts to regulate the possession of guns and ammunition, some 20,000 weapons were obtained in this manner. »

Members of the Rustington LDV, which later became part of the 6th Sussex (Arundel) Battalion Home Guard, pictured during a march in the summer of 1940.
(Courtesy of Mrs Mary Taylor)

ABOVE: A pair of slip-on shoulder titles for the LDV. (Historic Military Press)

Examples of the ingenuity and resourcefulness of many LDV or Home Guard units abound. The 49th Lancashire Battalion, for its part, borrowed a quantity of old Snider rifles from the Belle-vue Zoological Gardens in Manchester. These rifles had already seen service in the Crimea and Indian Mutiny campaigns. The 55th County of Lancaster Battalion armed each man on duty with a spear and a heavily weighted truncheon made by the employees of the Manchester Collieries Ltd. A Marylebone Company of the LDV scrounged four dozen .303 rifles from the Drury Lane Theatre where they had been used as props in a patriotic play. The 11th Salop Battalion, in declining the use of an ancient muzzle-loader, did accept a quantity of old service revolvers.

What rifles the War Office could spare were issued at first to those areas considered to be most at risk of invasion or of parachutists. Consequently, among the first to be armed were the groups in Kent. For those waiting in the queue, improvisation was the order of the day.

DIAMOND SCRATCHES TO HELP BREAKING OF BOTTLE

FUSE

ABOVE: A wartime diagram depicting a typical Molotov Cocktail design. (Historic Military Press)

A member of the Local Defence Volunteers prepares to through a Molotov Cocktail. (Historic Military Press)

The 77th County of Lancaster Battalion "acquired" fifty Martini-Henry carbines from another local Boys' Brigade unit. The 8th Hampshire (Avon Valley) Battalion achieved the almost impossible and equipped its newly-formed Mobile Platoon with a Lewis machine-gun complete with a supply of ammunition – apparently one veteran's memento of the First World War. The 30th Middlesex Battalion was less fortunate and could only parade with broom handles.

THE MOLOTOV COCKTAIL

Perhaps the only weapon available to many units in any quantity in the early weeks of the LDV was the Molotov Cocktail. It was during the Russo-Finnish war that the name "Molotov Cocktail" first appeared in the British press, a reference to the then Russian Foreign Minister, Skriabin Molotov.

ABOVE: A development of the relatively simple and easy to manufacture Molotov Cocktail was the No.76 Grenade. First demonstrated by the manufacturer, Albright & Wilson of Oldbury, on July 29, 1940, the No.76 Grenade, also commonly known as the A.W. Bomb or SIP Grenade (Self Igniting Phosphorus), was soon being issued to the Home Guard. By August 1941, well over 6,000,000 had been manufactured. The examples seen here were unearthed in their original wooden case close to former Home Guard positions near Arundel in West Sussex, the picture taken prior to their disposal. (Historic Military Press)

One of the first official mentions regarding the British use of this weapon was made on June 5, 1940, at a meeting of senior LDV officials. General Ironside, the newly appointed Commander-in-Chief Home Forces, addressed the gathering. Discussing the desperate situation in terms of weapons available to the newly formed LDV, he said: "I want also to develop this thing they developed in Finland, called the Molotov Cocktail. It is a bottle filled with resin, petrol and tar, which if thrown on top of a tank will ignite, and if you throw half a dozen more on it you have them cooked. It is quite an effective thing. If you can use your ingenuity, I give you a picture of a [road] block, with two houses close to the block overlooking it. Out of the top window is the place to drop these things on the tank as it passes the block. It may stop it for two minutes there, but it will be quite effective."

The comments made by General Ironside were taken on board by those present and disseminated down through the chain of command. Some days later Major W J C Kendall undertook a briefing of the Section Leaders of the Malvern LDV. Having repeated the words of General Ironside almost to the letter, Kendall went on to add: "This is a method of delaying the progress of the enemy tank while the Military authorities are getting to us. It is not necessary to effect complete annihilation, but to do anything which will cause delay is the real object."

Another of the early official references to this weapon appeared in July 1940. Local Defence Volunteers Instruction No.8 stated: "From the moment that enemy tanks are located they must be harried, hunted, sniped and ambushed without respite until they are destroyed. Goliath was slain by David's sling,

LDV recruits learning rifle drill at Buckhurst Hill, Essex, on July 1, 1940. (via Historic Military Press)

"During the Molotov Cocktail boom, we made our own missiles out of beer bottles."

and the lessons of Spain and Finland confirm that tanks can be destroyed by men who have bravery, resource and determination to do so."

Captain R. Baker of the Bexley LDV recalled being ordered to conjure-up his unit's armoury of Molotov Cocktails: "The Group Commander produced a bottle (with a patent top) and gave me orders to have several hundreds of these filled with a mixture of tar and petrol or paraffin ready for throwing in case of need at enemy tanks or the like. Owing to the slow supply of official bottles we had to get some from other sources.

"Consequently, on [a] Sunday morning, I went round the village on a farm cart collecting any old used whisky and soft drink bottles – beer bottles being too hard for easy breakage. Several hundred potential missiles were thus collected. The making of the mixture was carried out in a wood with the aid of a twig fire for boiling the tar, which was necessary in order to make it mix well."

In many cases, much effort would also be expended in an attempt to achieve the perfect "lob" of a Molotov Cocktail, as Captain Baker also recalled: "Wooden bottles were made for use in practise throwing, and as a target a tank was drawn in chalk on the wall of a disused house. Points were given for the best hits registered at 'vulnerable' parts. Later, an old car was brought, fitted and covered in sheet iron, and towed along a quiet road – Molotov throwers hiding either side ready to throw as the tank-like device passed along. During many of these practices, actual air raids were taking place, thereby giving an excellent touch of realism."

A volunteer with 'A' (Wilmington) Company, 'B' (Hailsham) Battalion East Sussex LDV describes yet another, though very similar, exercise: "During the Molotov

Cocktail boom, we made our own missiles out of beer bottles [the unit's HQ was, most conveniently, located at the Black Horse Inn in the down-land village of Wilmington]. We borrowed a dilapidated raking machine to represent a Hun tank. Then eight of us in turn would pull it across a field as fast as we could, while the others chucked the firebombs from behind a hedge. We had a competition with some officers of the Cheshire Regiment to see who could get the most hits. We won handsomely."

SUPPORT FROM THE UNITED STATES

As the first of the British appeals for weapons were being made, a number of Americans began watching the course of the war with increasing alarm and despondency. Some felt that Britain would surely fall – some, but by no means all. Declaring himself to be in the latter camp was one William Allen White. White was the editor of a Kansas small-town daily paper, the *Emporia Gazette*, and felt that America should do what it could to aid the defence of Britain.[2] »

ABOVE: Two examples of the commercially published manuals that were produced for members of the LDV and Home Guard. (Historic Military Press)

Utilising his position as a voice of the American Mid-West, White joined forces with other like-minded Americans and the "American Committee for the Defense of British Homes" was born. At its first meeting, the Committee formulated a proposal which, simply put, was to gather as many guns as possible from American citizens and ship them to the United Kingdom – without charge to the latter. The main Committee established itself in New York; in time it would be supported by some 364 local Committees across the United States.

Full-page adverts were taken out by the Committee, often without charge to it, in the national press, as well as more specialised publications. One such appeal can be seen in the November 1940 issue of the *American Rifleman* magazine. This was a well-targeted appeal, for this magazine was the official journal of the National Rifle Association of America. On page six can be found the headline "Send a gun to defend a British home". The advert went on to explain that "British civilians, faced with the threat of invasion, desperately need arms for the defense of their homes". It further explained that the Committee had "organised to collect gifts of pistols, rifles, revolvers, shotguns [and] binoculars from American civilians who wish to answer the call."[3]

There was no stipulation on what weapons would, or would not, be accepted – just that they had to be capable of firing and, where possible, come supplied with twenty rounds of ammunition. The donations came from a variety of individuals – from game-hunters to schoolboy rifle club members. Some of the weapons were old frontier buffalo guns; some were dated 1873; and others were long-rifles that had seen use in Louisiana during the American Civil War. One of the very first weapons handed over, at a carefully orchestrated

ceremony, was the former American President "Teddy" Roosevelt's favourite hunting rifle. The donor at the ceremony was his wife, Mrs Kermit Roosevelt.

In an unusual twist of fate, it would even be the case where one Home Guard unit donated weapons to arm another. In the First World War the district of Scarsdale, New York, established its own Home Guard, purchasing weapons with which to arm themselves. Many of the surviving members of this group turned over their rifles to the local Committee, asking that they be sent to their, more modern, British namesake.

Some of the items were also found to be of unusual interest. One gun expert who checked over some of the firearms donated later recalled that he had seen "a .41 Colt double-action model, a favourite type of none other than Billy the Kid… a Model 1873 Winchester .44-.40, the kind which Buffalo Bill used to shoot glass balls in a performance for Queen Victoria... and a single-action Colt .45, the six-shooter of song and story of our early West and the favourite ordnance of Wild Bill Hickok!" Another firearm of interest that found its way across the Atlantic was linked to Annie Oakley, the famous markswoman of the

Members of the Rustington LDV pictured during a parade with their first issue of rifles. (Courtesy of Mrs Mary Taylor)

Victorian era who had once undertaken a tour of England. She once owned an expensive English-made Greener shotgun that had subsequently been purchased in Chicago by C.B. Spears in 1892; it was presented to the Committee by his daughter.

To each weapon would be attached two labels – one bearing the name and address of the donor, the second detailing the specifications of the weapon. Some also bore messages of support. These tags enabled recipients in the UK to acknowledge their gratitude. Volunteer C.N. Galer, serving in the Sunbeam-Talbot factory Home Guard, penned a letter of appreciation to the Committee: "Please accept our grateful thanks for your generous help at what is probably the gravest hour in the history of this Country. Your weapons have found their way to our Factory [Home] Guard – a company of workmen, well-trained, keen

ABOVE: A representation of how a typical LDV member might have looked in late July 1940. He is wearing the denim uniform that was first issued in May 1940 – on the 22nd of that month Sir Edward Grigg announced that 90,000 sets of this uniform had already been issued. Army Council Instructions dated June 24, 1940, confirmed that each member of the LDV would be provided with this uniform, along with a service respirator, a steel helmet, a field service cap, and a field dressing. He is armed with a P17 .300 Enfield rifle.
(Historic Military Press)

RIGHT: A re-enactment of a member of the Home Guard on duty, in his LDV-issue denims, with a shot-gun. He is holding a shot-gun cartridge that has been officially issued by the War Department, details of which were included in Local Defence Volunteers Instructions No.9, which was published in July 1940.
(Historic Military Press)

SEND A GUN TO DEFEND A BRITISH HOME

British civilians, faced with threat of invasion, desperately need arms for the defense of their homes.

THE AMERICAN COMMITTEE FOR DEFENSE OF BRITISH HOMES

has organized to collect gifts of

PISTOLS—RIFLES—REVOLVERS SHOTGUNS—BINOCULARS

from American civilians who wish to answer the call and aid in defense of British homes.

These arms are being shipped, with the consent of the British Government, to
CIVILIAN COMMITTEE FOR PROTECTION OF HOMES
BIRMINGHAM, ENGLAND
The members of which are Wickham Steed, Edward Hulton, and Lord Davies

YOU CAN AID

by sending any arms or binoculars you can spare to

AMERICAN COMMITTEE FOR
DEFENSE OF BRITISH HOMES
C. Suydam Cutting, *Chairman*
ROOM 100
10 WARREN STREET, NEW YORK, N. Y.

ABOVE: An appeal that was placed in the American Press by the American Committee for the Defense of British Homes. This example appeared in the November 1940 issue of *American Rifleman* magazine. This was the official journal of the National Rifle Association of America, from whose members more than 7,000 weapons were donated, most of which ended up in the hands of the Home Guard. (By kind permission of the National Rifle Association of America)

MANUAL OF SMALL ARMS AND SPECIAL WEAPONS

1/-

COLT, WEBLEY SMITH & WESSON
LUGER, MAUSER REVOLVERS & AUTOMATIC PISTOLS

FULL DETAILS ON
LOADING
FIRING
STOPPAGES
IMMEDIATE ACTION
STRIPPING &
ASSEMBLING

"BOYS"
ANTI-TANK GUN
HAND GRENADES
NORTHOVER PROJECTOR
ETC.
ETC.

ETC. ETC.

For Home Guard & Service Use

BERNARDS, (Publishers,) LTD.
77, THE GRAMPIANS, WESTERN GATE, LONDON, W.6.

ABOVE: A copy of the *Manual of Small Arms and Special Weapons* which was published by Bernards for use by the Home Guard. As can be seen, it includes sections on an eclectic selection of pistols and revolvers such as the Colt, Webley, Smith & Wesson, Luger, and Mauser revolvers – all of which are likely to have found their way into LDV and Home Guard use in the summer of 1940. (Historic Military Press)

ABOVE: Local Defence Volunteers being inspected by senior officers, namely General Nation and Major Hughman, at their post in Whitehall, June 21, 1940. (via Historic Military Press)

and even anxious for the opportunity to test its strength against the superlatively equipped German parachute troops, who, it is said, intend to land and take possession of Factories such as this. I can assure you that the men who will handle your gifts will give a good account of themselves against any attackers – in the interim, they will be used for anti-sabotage precautions."

Volunteer W. Rough of Hare Hatch, near Twyford in Berkshire, wrote to the Committee to thank them for six Colt revolvers that had just been issued to his unit. Rough ended his letter by saying that "these guns are being used by horsemen who have formed one of the few mounted patrols in England, and who nightly patrol the territory over which they once hunted".

Another volunteer, one D. Muir serving in the St. Albans Home Guard, noted the following: "I write to thank you for a Colt .38 which I have received and to assure you that if the invasion we have been promised occurs it will be put to good use. I carried a Colt during four years of the last war when I served in one of the Highland battalions. I know therefore what a fine weapon it is."

Over time the response to the Committee's appeals in the United States was truly impressive. By early 1941 tens of thousands of weapons had been donated – far more than the similar appeal in the United Kingdom had produced. In June the following year, at which point the Committee was considering the need to continue operating, it announced that it had shipped a staggering 5,133 rifles and shotguns, 20,100 pistols and revolvers, 110 Thompson sub-machineguns and 2,042,291 rounds of ammunition across the Atlantic. The members of the National Rifle Association of America alone would hand over an estimated 7,000 pieces.

It was not only weapons that poured into the collection centres – each delivery also brought stopwatches, steel helmets (of various vintages), and binoculars. By the time that this side of the Committee's work ended, it had sent some 2,993 binoculars and telescopes, 379 stopwatches and 16,322 steel helmets to the United Kingdom.

THE HOME GUARD

For their part, as weapons gradually became available the LDV volunteers declared that they were "itching" to get to grips with the enemy. This sentiment was voiced in the Commons by Colonel Josiah Wedgwood, »

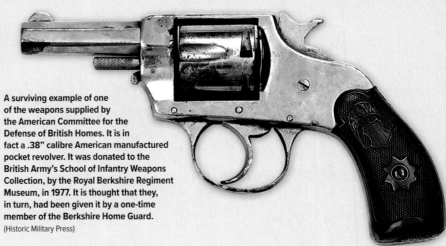

A surviving example of one of the weapons supplied by the American Committee for the Defense of British Homes. It is in fact a .38" calibre American manufactured pocket revolver. It was donated to the British Army's School of Infantry Weapons Collection, by the Royal Berkshire Regiment Museum, in 1977. It is thought that they, in turn, had been given it by a one-time member of the Berkshire Home Guard. (Historic Military Press)

As well as weapons, the LDV and Home Guard received various forms of transport vehicles in the summer of 1940. Here men of the Littlehampton (Sussex) Home Guard parade their despatch riders' motorbikes on the sports ground of St. Nicholas' School, Granville Road, Littlehampton. Note the mix of LDV and Home Guard signs. The photograph was provided by Ernest Wilson, who is sitting on the motorbike on the far right with his goggles on his head. (Courtesy of Ernest Wilson)

MP for Newcastle-Under-Lyme, who declared: "The Local Defence Force [sic] is not a mere stepchild of the War Office but is genuinely intended to act in the service of this country, not as an extra policeman to guard the German soldiers when they march through London, but as an active Defence Force, that this Force, if it cannot get rifles, will at least have hand grenades and that it will not be required to retreat but to hold the country."[4]

In a bid to calm the growing discontent, the War Office announced that volunteers would be entitled to steel helmets, service respirators, greatcoats, leather gaiters, boots, leather belts, and haversacks. Also stated by the other Joint Under-Secretary of State for War, Lord Henry Croft, was the fact that, "The Army Council regard the Local Defence Volunteers as a really vital part of our essential defences. It is no mere outlet of patriotic emotion which we are endeavouring to recruit, but a fighting force which may be at death grips with the enemy next week, or even to-morrow. That is the attitude of the War Office towards this force, and for that reason it has been placed

ABOVE: A cartoon that illustrates the often rudimentary and haphazard supply of weapons to the LDV in the early days and weeks. (Historic Military Press)

under the command of the Commander-in-Chief of the Home Forces, and a leader of the calibre of Sir Edmund Ironside has been appointed."[5]

At last, the LDV was being accorded the distinction of being fully recognised as an integral part of the defence of the realm. As more weapons became available and the training became more advanced, the LDV was genuinely turning into a serious fighting force. Churchill, however, was still concerned with reports of low morale in the force, which he ascribed to its uninspiring title. In fact, the LDV had already been labelled "Look, Duck, Vanish" by some. A new name was needed, one which described its role as an important part of the nations' defence. From July 23, 1940, therefore, the Local Defence Force officially became the Home Guard.

ABOVE: Not only have these men of a Berkshire LDV unit been equipped with an improvised armoured car, they are also armed with the 'Molotov Slinger' that can be seen in the foreground. Based in Maidenhead, their unit was commanded by Colonel W.H. Tickler, the owner of a well-known Berkshire fruit-preserving firm, who placed the staff and facilities of his factory at the disposal of the battalion. One of the men in the turret has what appears to be a Luger fitted with a snail drum magazine. (Historic Military Press)

NOTES

1. Charles Graves, p.43.
2. *Picture Post*; Volume 9, No.9., November 30, 1940.
3. *The American Rifleman*; Volume 88, No.11. November 1940.
4. *Hansard*, vol 362 cc51-64.
5. *Hansard*, vol 116 cc467-96.

The Home Guard: A Timeline

The Home Guard was, and remains, one of the most fantastic military forces ever raised. History can provide few, if any, parallels to its speed of recruitment, enthusiasm and numbers. In this timeline we explore some of the key moments and events in the history of the United Kingdom's largest ever volunteer army.

1939

October 8
Winston Churchill, First Lord of the Admiralty, wrote to the Lord Privy Seal, Samuel Hoare, proposing the creation of a 'home guard' force of some 500,000 men.

1940

May 11
A meeting was held, at which the War Office and the Ministry of Home Security were represented, to discuss the matter of Home Defence. Present was General Sir Walter Kirke, Commander-in-Chief of Home Forces, who had already been considering the formation of a new Home Defence force.

May 12
General Kirke's plans were presented at a meeting in the War Office. The name Local Defence Volunteers (LDV) was approved.

May 12
Having replaced Oliver Stanley as the Secretary of State for War on 11 May, Anthony Eden, in one of his first acts in this new role, sought, and obtained, final Cabinet approval for the formation of the LDV.

May 13
Using notes provided from previous meetings and discussions, the Secretary of State for War drafted the speech that would call for volunteers for the LDV.

May 14
It was agreed on this date that the LDV "would form part of the armed forces of the Crown, and would be subject to military law".

May 14
Anthony Eden made his immortal broadcast on the BBC announcing the formation of the LDV and called for volunteers to come forward. »

Local Defence Volunteers on parade. The original caption to this image, dated June 22, 1940, states: "London's Defence Volunteers shown during a recruiting parade and inspection, as they marched past Maj Gen Sir Cecil Pereira, London area organiser."
(Historic Military Press)

May 17
During a Privy Council meeting at Buckingham Palace, King George VI approved an Order in Council dealing with the establishment of the LDV.

May 20
It was confirmed in Parliament that more than 250,000 men had already enlisted in the LDV.

May 22
It was announced in the House of Commons that 90,000 sets of denim overalls had been issued to the LDV, and that 250,000 field service caps were available. A similar number of armbands had been ordered.

May 26
The Commander-in-Chief Home Forces asked all those in possession of 12-bore cartridges to hand as many as possible into their nearest police station for redistribution to the LDV.

June 2
The LDV suffered its first casualty when Volunteer Thomas Lyon was killed by the accidental discharge of a rifle in Dumbarton.

June 5
General Ironside, Commander-in-Chief Home Forces, held a meeting of leaders of the LDV. During this, he confirmed that some 80,000 rifles had already been issued, but urged the new units to make use of the Molotov Cocktail.

June 24
LDV appointment markings, or insignia, were set down in Army Council Instruction No.653. These were as follows: Zone Commander (four dark blue cloth stripes on each shoulder strap); Battalion Commander (three dark blue cloth stripes on each shoulder strap); Company Commander (two dark blue cloth stripes); Platoon Commander (one dark blue cloth stripe on each shoulder strap); and Section Commander (three worsted chevrons).

ABOVE: **Members of the Waterlooville, Hampshire, Home Guard parading for the National Day of Prayer, held on September 8, 1940.** (Historic Military Press)

June 24
The various county Territorial Associations were made responsible for the administration of the LDV in their areas, taking charge of the drawing, distribution and issuing of all uniform and equipment.

June 25
Eden announced in the House of Commons that the LDV's uniform was intended to consist of one suit of overalls of design similar to that of battle dress, a field service cap, and an armlet bearing the letters 'L.D.V.'".

June 26
Churchill wrote to the Secretary of State for War suggesting that the LDV be renamed the Home Guard.

June 30
Eden further announced that members of

the LDV/Home Guard were to be issued with boots as and when stocks permitted.

July 13
During an air raid on the night of the 12th/13th, Volunteer G Jones, 3rd Monmouthshire (Newport) Battalion, was on duty at a defence post when it was bombed. Despite the dangers from falling glass and other debris, he went to the assistance of his colleagues. For his actions that night, Jones was awarded the Military Medal. He was the first, and only, Local Defence Volunteer/Home Guard to be decorated in this manner.

July 20
The King inspected some 2,000 members of the LDV at Woodford in Essex. One of the men he was introduced to was Volunteer Henry Kenny, who had been awarded the Victoria Cross for his actions near Loos in 1915.

July 23
The LDV was officially renamed the Home Guard.

August 3
The Home Guard was affiliated to county regiments; permission was given to wear regimental cap badges and battledress. Shoulder titles and abbreviated county and battalion numbers were adopted to differentiate volunteers from regular and territorial forces.

August 7
Following a question raised by Lieutenant Colonel Acland-Troyte, the Secretary of State for War stated that the approximate cost of supplying the new armbands for the Home Guard, following the change of name, was approximately £3,500.

ABOVE: **Men of a Yorkshire Home Guard battalion ambushing their armoured car during exercises on the Yorkshire Dales. Note that a Molotov cocktail can be seen exploding in the road behind the armoured car.** (Historic Military Press)

August 7
The Ministry of Food was asked to arrange for Home Guard units to be supplied with extra tea and sugar rations at posts which had to be permanently manned.

August 10
The King attended West Wickham in Kent to watch a 3,000-strong force of the Home Guard "conduct various exercises". An official note made at the time states: "The majority of the troops were fully armed and equipped, while the soldierly bearing and steadiness of all was especially noteworthy".

August 15
Army Council Instruction No.924 set down the ranks for the Home Guard. In descending order these were: Zone Commander; Group Commander; Battalion Commander; Company Commander; Platoon Commander; Section Commander; and Squad Commander. There was also the rank of Private.

proportion of uniforms of larger dimensions?" Sir Edward Grigg, Under-Secretary of State for War, replied that, indeed, larger uniforms had been ordered.

October 16
During an air raid on the night of the 15th/16th, Section Commander George Inwood, 10th Birmingham (Public Utilities) Battalion, lost his life attempting to rescue a group of survivors trapped in a gas-filled cellar. He was posthumously awarded the recently-instituted George Cross. He was the first Home Guard to be recognised in this manner.

November 5
In a speech detailing the "war situation", Churchill confirmed that there were some "1,700,000 men in the Home Guard". He added that "nearly 1,000,000 of the Home Guard have rifles or machine guns", and that "nearly half of the whole Home Guard are veteran soldiers of the last war".

ABOVE: The Home Guard makes the German press – as this page from the issue of the *Berliner Illustrite Zeitung* of September 19, 1940 shows. As well as depicting the same armoured car being 'attacked' by the men of a Yorkshire unit (opposite page), it also has an image showing Winston Churchill viewing activity in the Channel from an observation post at Dover Castle, during his tour of defences on August 28, 1940, and details and weapons linked to the Home Guard. The latter includes a drawing of a Molotov Cocktail. (Historic Military Press)

Martin was the oldest Home Guard fatality of the war. Both men were aged 68. Langdale, serving in the 53rd Surrey (Weston Green) Battalion, was killed on 4 October 1940. The Commonwealth War Graves Commission notes that Langdale was "a veteran of the South African War".

January 9
Winston Churchill inspected the 1st American Motorized Squadron at Horse Guards Parade, London. »

ABOVE: Members of the Montgomeryshire (Llandyssil) Home Guard pictured after a Church Parade at Llandyssil Parish Church on September 14, 1940. Note that a number of the men are wearing their First World War medals. (National Library of Wales)

September 25
This was the worst day for fatalities suffered by the Home Guard during the war. A total of seventeen men were killed during German air raids, all of whom were serving in the 13th Gloucestershire Battalion.

October 13
Recruitment into the Home Guard was temporarily suspended due to a continuing shortage of uniforms, weapons and equipment.

October 15
The Secretary of State for War was asked whether he was aware that "the physical dimensions of a proportion of the Home Guard are greater than those customary in the Regular Army; and whether he will make arrangements for the production of a

November 19
Sir Edward Grigg confirmed that there was "something like 1,200 battalions, 5,000 companies, 25,000 platoons" in the Home Guard. "It is an enormous Force," he added, "five or six times as great as the Territorial Army". He also commented that "No one will claim for the Home Guard that it is a miracle of organisation… but many would claim that it is a miracle of improvisation."

1941

January 2
Serving with the 16th Glamorganshire (Cardiff) Battalion, Volunteer Walter Martin was killed in an air raid on this night. Along with Volunteer Charles Langdale,

ABOVE: On May 20, 1941, to mark the first anniversary of the formation of the Home Guard, the force was given the honour of mounting guard at Buckingham Palace. This was repeated again on May 20, 1943. (Historic Military Press)

January 21

It was confirmed in *The London Gazette* on this date that 16-year-old Volunteer P D Willeringhaus, 6th Battalion, 'P' Zone, London Home Guard, had been Mentioned in Despatches for his gallantry whilst serving as a despatch rider during an air raid on the Streatham area. He was the only Home Guard to be honoured in this manner in the war.

January 22

The award of the George Medal to Section Leader A H Tilyard-Burrows was announced in *The London Gazette*, this being the first time for a member of the Home Guard. At the time of his actions during and after an air raid on September 21, 1940, Tilyard-Burrows was serving in the Vickers Armstrong Aircraft Factory Unit. A total of 13 George Medals were awarded to members of the Home Guard during the war.

February 12

Home Guard officers were granted commissions. Confirmed in the Home Guard Officers' Commissions Order, which was passed on this date, this was with retrospective effect to February 1.

ABOVE: A pair of Home Guards pictured during training. The Corporal on the left appears to be equipped with a Lewis machine-gun. A handwritten note on the rear states: "Wednesday, July 15, 1942. Anti-tank training." From information provided with the image, it is believed that the Home Guards are from a unit in the Winchester, Hampshire, area. (Historic Military Press)

March 13

Revised Home Guard rank badges were set down in a War Office telegram on this date, the information being confirmed in Army Council Instruction No.623 of April 24, 1941. These were, in effect, generally the same as the Regular Army from Brigadier down.

March 14

The Home Guard suffered its third highest fatality toll on this day. A total of ten men were killed in air raids, eight of whom were serving in the 4th City of Glasgow Battalion.

April 2

Home Guard shoulder titles were officially authorised by the War Office.

ABOVE: Members of the Cheshire Home Guard pictured on the Sten gun range that was established at Vittoria Dock, Birkenhead. It opened in May 1943. (Historic Military Press)

April 2

Based on plans drawn up by Colonel W C Harthill, Medical Advisor to G.H.Q. Home Forces, the Home Guard Medical Service was instigated on this date.

April 16

With fifteen casualties, this date marked the second worst day for fatalities in the history of the Home Guard. Of the fifteen men who died that day, eleven were members of the 57th Surrey (Mitcham) Battalion – all killed by German bombs. A further two members of this battalion would succumb to their injuries in the following days.

May 7

Army Council Instruction No.721 stipulated that a Home Guard unit may play the Regimental March of the county regiment it was affiliated to.

May 14

To mark the first anniversary of the establishment of the Home Guard, the organisation was given the privilege of mounting guard at Buckingham Palace.

July 1

The first announcement of awards to Home Guard personnel in the half-yearly lists began on this date, the King's Birthday Honours 1941.

July 17

Private Donald Long, 24th Warwickshire (Birmingham) Battalion, was killed during an air raid on this date. Only 15 years old, he was, according to the Commonwealth War Graves Commission's records, the youngest Home Guard casualty of the Second World War. Private Arthur Owens was even younger, being just 14 years old, when he was killed during

ABOVE: Members of one or more of the Brighton Home Guard units on parade. Brighton fielded a number of Home Guard units, including the 10th Sussex (East Brighton) Battalion, the 15th Sussex (West Brighton) Battalion and the 11th Sussex (39 GPO) Battalion. (Historic Military Press)

"I had not got the heart to shoot him, so I stepped back and let him in."

ABOVE: Members of the Rustington LDV enjoy a moment of relaxation in the summer of 1940. (Courtesy of Mrs Mary Taylor)

complete with maps, wireless sets and sabotage equipment across the Midlands on the night of August 13/14, 1940, with a further 59 the following day. Understandably, with "parachute fever" spreading uncontrollably across the nation, any unidentified object in the sky was thought to be a parachutist.

A strong north-westerly gale on August 20, 1940 caused a number of barrage balloons protecting the passage of the River Mersey, to break free. One of these caused chaos as far afield as Rutland where it was thought to be an enemy parachutist. The balloon was chased by Colonel Ogilvy-Dalgleish, commander of the Rutland Home Guard, and a unit of the 50th (Holding) Battalion Royal Scots Fusiliers was also put on alert, with the troops embussed and ready to move off. At one stage the colonel was informed by the police, in turn acting on a "reliable source", that parachutists were dropping near Luffenham in an attempt to seize the airfield there. An hour later, his Home Guards reported that a barrage balloon had just come down near Ridlington and the panic

was over. Similar misidentified sightings were made by people across other counties as the balloons dropped to earth.

A similar dramatic message was received one night by the Anstey Home Guard that parachutes had been sighted in a field just outside the village. "We duly arrived at the field and peered gingerly over the hedge," recalled Home Guard Fred Jones. "Sure enough, there on the grass lay haphazard shapes of fabric, evidence of the enemy's descent from the skies. Abandoned parachutes? No, it had been a windy night and bed linen and clothes had been blown from a washing line."[4]

Likewise, on August 20, volunteer P S Wakefield of the Brush Works Home Guard was alerted following reports that 'parachutists' had been seen at Loughborough and Coalville: "All quiet today until 5pm when Capt Lewis rang up telling us to take special precautions as parachutists had landed at Quorn and in surrounding district. It was an inconvenient time of day, but I managed to collect 14 others as a scratch section to man our fire posts and the two main gates. We hadn't been there very long before Section Leader Van Zwannenberg reported he had seen a parachute come down in the Normanton direction. L.G. Reid arrived, got in touch with Capt C.K. Lewis our Company Commander. The three of us with W. Mercer drove over the hills to where the parachute had been reported.

"Nothing was to be seen until a huge barrage balloon came blowing along in the wind. Until it was quite near it looked remarkably like a parachute with a man on it, but balloon it was, like the one you saw earlier in the afternoon. After shorting the grid wires with its trailing wire, it shot up and disappeared into the clouds."[5] »

ABOVE: An early example of a printed Home Guard armband. (Richard Hunt Collection)

ABOVE MIDDLE: A member of No.2 Platoon, 'C' Company of the Rustington Home Guard, part of the 6th Sussex (Arundel) Battalion, pictured on patrol in the summer of 1940. He is accompanied by the unit's dog, 'Trip'. Note his helmet hung over his shoulder, the P.14 rifle and the bandolier of ammunition.
ABOVE: 'Trip' stands guard at the entrance to the headquarters of No.2 Platoon, 'C' Company of the Rustington Home Guard in the summer of 1940. (Both courtesy of Mrs Mary Taylor)

ABOVE: Men of the 47th County of London (London County Council) Battalion, on duty in a guard post outside County Hall, watch as one of their armoured cars passes by during a patrol on August 23, 1940. On the wall behind the sentry post is a sign stating "This is not a public shelter – the nearest is at Stangate opposite St. Thomas's Hospital". (Historic Military Press)

Reports of enemy landings came thick and fast throughout the summer. Another such incident was recalled by an officer in the 14th Hampshire (Fareham) Battalion: "One September morning… an alarm was given that gliders had landed near Titchfield. A section of men in a trench at Sandringham Lane were standing to as dawn broke.

"It was a misty morning and they heard the tramp of feet and saw four figures approaching them through the mist. The Corporal in charge gave correct fire orders: range, direction, and to hold fire until his command –

"Just then the mist lifted and they saw the four figures had a large body on the top. It turned out to be a horse and the cropping of the grass had made the sound of marching feet." What must have been a tense few moments ended without further incident.

TAKEN PRISONER

With the Battle of Britain raging overhead, there were indeed some parachutists for the Home Guard to greet. Two days before Wakefield and his colleagues had responded to the report of Fallschirmjäger landing between Loughborough and Coalville, the RAF's Fighter Command suffered what came to be known as the "Hardest Day" – Sunday, August 18. Pilot Officer Kenneth 'Hawkeye' Lee was flying in the centre of 501 Squadron when enemy fighters pounced. Lee later recalled what happened next: "A bullet hit my leg, which shot up in the air, and then another explosive bullet struck the metal behind me and filled my shoulder with little fragments, and a moment later a big burst of oil, smoke and flames came up between my legs from the main tank.

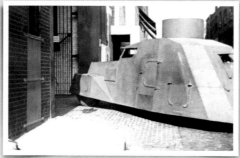

ABOVE: Another of the LCC battalions' armoured cars is pictured entering the area of County Hall. The original caption suggests that the donor vehicle was a Rolls-Royce limousine from the official fleet. (Historic Military Press)

"I tried the controls, but it was obvious my Hurricane was finished – there was too much smoke and flames. So, with the experience of my previous effort when I had baled out and struck the tailplane, I rolled the aircraft on its back and pushed the stick forwards and released my Sutton harness before pulling the canopy back. I had forgotten to disconnect the oxygen, which I quickly did, and baled out."[6]

Lee slowly descended to earth, eventually landing in a cornfield near Whitstable. It was then that he encountered a member of the local Home Guard unit: "I felt my flying-boot was filling up with blood; it was like wearing a wet Wellington. I was immediately 'captured' by an old chap who was wearing a uniform cap from the 1914-18 War. He levelled a rifle at me, which I later learned he had captured from the Turks at Gallipoli. I was out of uniform and wasn't carrying any ID, and he wouldn't believe that I was British… They brought up an ambulance eventually. I was able to hobble to the transport, and was taken to Leeds Castle, where they took the bullet and shrapnel out and patched me up."

For those fighter pilots whose first language was not English, such situations often presented added complications. A Pole, Pilot Officer Marian Pisarek had been posted to the Hurricane-equipped 303 Squadron which was based at Northolt. When he scrambled on September 7, it marked his first operational sortie with the RAF. "In a flight of three machines," notes one account, "Pisarek and his colleagues attacked bombers before being attacked themselves by fighters. After hitting and, it appeared, destroying one fighter, Pisarek's own machine was hit and started issuing smoke and went out of control."

With little option, Pisarek baled out. "[He] was floating down towards Alderton Hill, Loughton, watched by a number of residents. He landed in a tree and became entangled in its branches. He had managed to free himself just as he was taken 'prisoner' by a member of the local Home Guard (Charles Cranwell) and an approaching mob of locals. Pisarek's identity

ABOVE: King George VI talking to a member of the Home Guard during an inspection in Kent, August 10, 1940. (via Historic Military Press)

"I was immediately 'captured' by an old chap who was wearing a uniform cap from the 1914-18 War."

BELOW: Members of the Rustington Home Guard, part of the 6th Sussex (Arundel) Battalion, pose for the camera beside a Junkers Ju 87 Stuka. This was Ju 87 B-1, coded S2+JN, Wk. Nr. 5167, of 5/StG 77, which came down at Ham Manor Golf Course, Angmering, West Sussex, at 14.23 hours on August 18, 1940. (Courtesy of Mrs Mary Taylor)

ABOVE: A set of training notes written by Private Herbert Macartney of the 52nd Surrey (Surbiton) Battalion, Home Guard, during instruction on the methods of rescue of aircrew in crashed aircraft. (Historic Military Press)

card proved him to be friend rather than foe, but his thick foreign accent made it preferable that the safety of the police station be sought."[7]

Another 303 Squadron pilot to suffer such a fate was Flying Officer Wojciech Januszewicz, this time on the afternoon of September 26. Januszewicz had scrambled in the same section as his commanding officer, Squadron Leader R G Kellett, and which subsequently intercepted a force of Heinkel He 111s unloading their deadly cargo on the Southampton area. In the subsequent engagement, Januszewicz's Hurricane, P3544 coded RF-H, was either damaged or malfunctioned. It was observed by a fellow Pole, Flying Officer Bohdan Grzeszczak, to have "let down its undercarriage and landed in a field".

One of those on the ground watching events unfold was Platoon Commander F M Hughes of the 14th Hampshire (Fareham) Battalion – a unit we encountered a little earlier. He later submitted a report detailing what followed: "During the air warfare overhead, a Polish pilot, flying a Spitfire [sic], was forced down near Charity Farm [some accounts give this as Wyton Farm], about 16.00 hours in the afternoon. I rushed up there with a car, thinking it might be 'Jerry.' Before I could get there one of my H.G. from the farm was on the spot covering the pilot with a 12-bore. Unfortunately, the pilot could only speak a few words of English, which failed to convince the fellow with the shotgun.

"I immediately placed a double guard over the aeroplane and escorted the pilot to Charity Farm, where we rang up H.Q., who relieved our guard. The pilot was entertained to tea at Charity Farm."[8]

Another pilot to come into contact with the Home Guard after baling out was Pilot Officer Bernard Brown, a New Zealander serving in 72 Squadron. His Battle of Britain effectively ended on September 23, after he was shot down over Gravesend: "A cannon shell entered the cockpit, hit Brown's left leg and destroyed the throttle assembly. With no control over the aircraft and also wounded in an elbow, Brown baled out and landed on marshy ground near Eastchurch, where, he later reported, he was menaced by a Home Guardsman with a rifle, before an RAF vehicle arrived."[9]

In some cases, an unfortunate descending 'friendly' pilot might even be fired upon by those on the ground. This is exactly what happened to 19-year-old Pilot Officer J F D 'Tim' Elkington of No.1 Squadron after he fell to the guns of a German fighter on August 16. Flying Hurricane P3173, he had been providing top cover when his squadron encountered 100 German aircraft in the vicinity of Portsmouth Harbour. Author Gordon Riley described what happened:

"In the ensuing melee, Tim never saw the aircraft that riddled his Hurricane with cannon shells – although, amazingly, his mother did. From nearby Hayling Island, and quite unaware that her son was involved, she watched the lone Hurricane pursued by three Bf 109s. A fuel tank exploded, peppering Tim with shrapnel; as he bailed [sic] out he forgot to disconnect his oxygen supply and the mask was subsequently ripped from his face – leaving a scar which he bears to this day.

"Tim lost consciousness and would have drifted out to sea and certain death if it had not been for the actions of his flight commander, F/Sgt Fred Berry, who followed him down and used the slipstream of his own Hurricane to blow Tim's parachute back towards land. Despite being fired on by the Home Guard, after landing at West Wittering Tim was taken to the Royal Sussex Hospital at Chichester, from where he was

put on sick leave and was sent to convalesce. Fred Berry was killed on 1 September, before Tim had a chance to thank him."[10]

A VICTORIA CROSS ACTION

Another 'target' was Flight Lieutenant James Brindley Nicolson, this time on Friday, August 16, 1940. Flying a Hurricane of 249 Squadron, he was involved in combat with Messerschmitt Bf 110s over Southampton when his aircraft was hit and set on fire. What happened next was revealed in a recording he subsequently made, and which was broadcast on the BBC in December 1940:

"I was still a long way from the squadron when suddenly, very close in rapid succession, I heard four big bangs. They were the loudest noises I had ever heard, and they had been made by four cannon shells from a Messerschmitt 110 hitting my machine. »

A portrait of Flight Lieutenant J B Nicolson. (Courtesy of Andy Saunders)

ABOVE: Flight Lieutenant J.B. Nicolson (centre) photographed just prior to his action on August 16, 1940, with Squadron Leader J Grandy (left), the commanding officer of 249 Squadron, and Pilot Officer E N Lohmeyer (right), the squadron adjutant. (Courtesy of Andy Saunders)

ABOVE: This drawing of Nicolson's Victoria Cross action was created at the request of the Ministry of Information for propaganda purposes during the Second World War. Moments later Nicolson would be fired upon by the Home Guard. (Historic Military Press)

"The first shell tore through the hood over my cockpit and sent splinters into my left eye. One splinter, I later discovered, nearly severed my eyelid. I couldn't see through that eye for blood. The second cannon shell struck my spare petrol tank and set it on fire. The third shell crashed into the cockpit and tore off my right trouser leg. The fourth shell struck the back of my left shoe. It shattered the heel of the shoe and made quite a mess of my left foot… I was just thinking about jumping out when suddenly a Messerschmitt 110 whizzed underneath me and got right in my gun sight…

"By this time, it was pretty hot inside my machine from the burst petrol tank. I couldn't see much flame, but I reckoned it was there alright. I remember looking once at my left hand, which was keeping the throttle open, which seemed to be in the fire itself and I could see the skin peeling off it, yet I had little pain. Unconsciously too, I had drawn my feet up under my parachute on the seat to escape the heat, I suppose."

Nicolson left us another personal testimony in the form of his personal Combat Report of the action. In this he noted the following: "I then abandoned aircraft with difficulty and after dropping some 5,000ft pulled cord – I was shot in the buttocks by an LDV just before landing."

ABOVE: The conversion of a civilian vehicle into a Home Guard armoured car is almost complete in the summer of 1940. The work seen here is being undertaken at the Berkshire factory of Colonel W H Tickler, the commanding officer of the Maidenhead Home Guard. (Historic Military Press)

ABOVE: The original caption, dated October 1, 1940, states that this image shows "Home Guards training with machine-guns, being put through a week's intensive training in the use of modern guns of various types, shown here with a Lewis anti-aircraft gun". It is known that the picture was taken at a Weapons Training School in Western Command. (Historic Military Press)

For his actions that day, Nicolson was awarded the Victoria Cross. He was Fighter Command's only VC recipient of the Battle of Britain and, indeed, of the whole war.

FACE TO FACE WITH THE ENEMY

On occasions, a member of the Home Guard found himself in the situation of encountering the enemy up close and personal. One of these instances is recounted in the *Western Times* of Friday, August 2, 1940: "After a crippled German bomber had skimmed the roof-top of his farm and crashed in a nearby field… a 47-year-old farmer, a member of the Home Guard, seized a double-barrelled shotgun and raced across the farmyard in his stockinged feet to capture the pilot as he attempted to escape after coming down by parachute. The pilot was the only survivor of a crew of four of a bomber which had been caught in the beams of a searchlight in endeavouring to escape from pursuing R.A.F. fighters. The other three occupants were found dead amid the wreckage.

"Mr. B.J. Parsons, who served for four years in France and Belgium with the Royal Engineers in the last war, said that when he heard a crash he looked out of his bedroom window and saw a figure scrambling down a narrow lane and, although he shouted several times, he received no reply. 'It is a wonder I did not shoot him then,' said Mr. Parsons. 'He was a bit contrary, and if he had moved his hands, I should have let him have it. My daughter, who had come on the scene, told me not to do it. I put on some clothes and caught the pilot as he was coming down the lane. He was terribly frightened because he had been told, he said, that if he came down in England, he would have his throat cut.'

ABOVE: Members of the machine-gun section of the Rustington Home Guard, part of the 6th Sussex (Arundel) Battalion, pose for the camera beside their weapons in the summer of 1940. (Courtesy of Mrs Mary Taylor)

"The farmer's 43-year-old wife, who is a mother of ten children, came downstairs in her nightdress and bathed and bandaged the young pilot's injuries. With his lacerated hand in an improvised sling the German sat down at the kitchen table and had a cup of tea and some cake, while wide-eyed youngsters crept downstairs to see the visitor that father had brought in.

"After the pilot had recovered, he was given a walking stick and, with Mr. Parsons still armed with his shotgun, walked two miles along country lanes to the village constable's house. The officer was out, and the farmer remained with the pilot and constable's wife until the police from headquarters arrived."

An examination of enemy losses in the Battle of Britain suggests that the aircraft involved might be a Heinkel He 111 of 1/KG 4. Coded 5J+AH, it crashed at Longfield Farm, near Smeatharpe in Devon, at 00.55 hours on July 26, 1940.

Whilst Farmer Parsons withstood the urge to open fire, his colleagues in the 5th Sussex (Worthing) Battalion were far less restrained,

for obvious reasons, when they swung into action a few days later on August 16. Their commanding officer, Lieutenant Colonel L M Kent, later provided the following account: "Six enemy 'planes were brought down on the South Coast, one of which passed over Sompting from the west using its machine-guns. Some ten men of the Sompting Platoon immediately seized their rifles and took up positions on the hillside adjacent to their post. The men held their fire until the target was within range. The 'plane seemed to hesitate, made a sharp turn and sprayed with machine-gun bullets the field where the men were stationed.

"No member of the Home Guard was hit, nor any of the farm workers who had taken refuge behind corn ricks, but it was evident that the 'plane had been hit, and after just missing the hilltop it crashed two miles away. Soldiers were quickly on the spot and took prisoner the crew, two of whom were wounded. On examination of the wrecked 'plane about fifteen rifle bullet holes in the fuselage were observed. This was the first,

and so far, only 'plane to be brought down by Home Guard action in this area."

Three Heinkel 111s came down in the area around Worthing area that afternoon. Based on the information provided by Lieutenant Colonel Kent, it is possible that the aircraft his men engaged was the He 111P, coded G1+HP of 6/KG 55, which crashed at Annington's Farm, Bramber, a short distance away on the other side of the South Downs from Sompting, at 17.15 hours.

TRAINING TAKES OVER

As the autumn faded into winter, invasion jitters gradually eased, at least until the spring. Churchill remarked to this effect in Parliament on November 6, when he announced that the 'invasion scare' had diminished. "But don't let us make the mistake of thinking that it has passed away," he added.

This meant that there was time for training to turn the, still-growing, Home Guard into a more efficient defence force. By the time that the 'invasion season' came around again, the men would be better equipped and prepared to face the threat.

NOTES

1. Charles Graves, *The Home Guard of Britain* (Fleet Street Press, London, 1943), p.89.
2. *Leicester Mercury*, June 13, 1940, quoted in Austin J Ruddy, *To The Last Round: The Leicestershire and Rutland Home Guard 1940-1945* (Breedon Books, Derby, 2007).
3. Dunstable Town Centre, 'Homeguard Memories', BBC People's War, Article ID: A3667584.
4. *Leicester Mercury*, May 2, 1990, quoted in Austin J Ruddy, ibid.
5. TNA WO 166/1222.
6. Quoted in Nick Thomas, *Kenneth 'Hawkeye' Lee DFC: Battle of Britain & Desert Air Force Fighter Ace* (Pen & Sword, Barnsley, 2011).
7. Anon, *Crashes and Mishaps 3*, published by North Weald Airfield Museum Archives.
8. Charles Graves, ibid, pp.215-6.
9. Gordon Riley, *Hawker Hurricane Survivors* (Grub Street, London, 2015), p.35.
10. Kenneth G Wynn, *Men of the Battle of Britain: A Supplementary Volume* (Frontline, Barnsley, 2020), p.13.

"I put on some clothes and caught the pilot as he was coming down the lane."

BELOW: A group of Home Guards pose for a unit photograph. Images such as this represent the largest part of the visual history of the Home Guard. (Richard Hunt Collection)

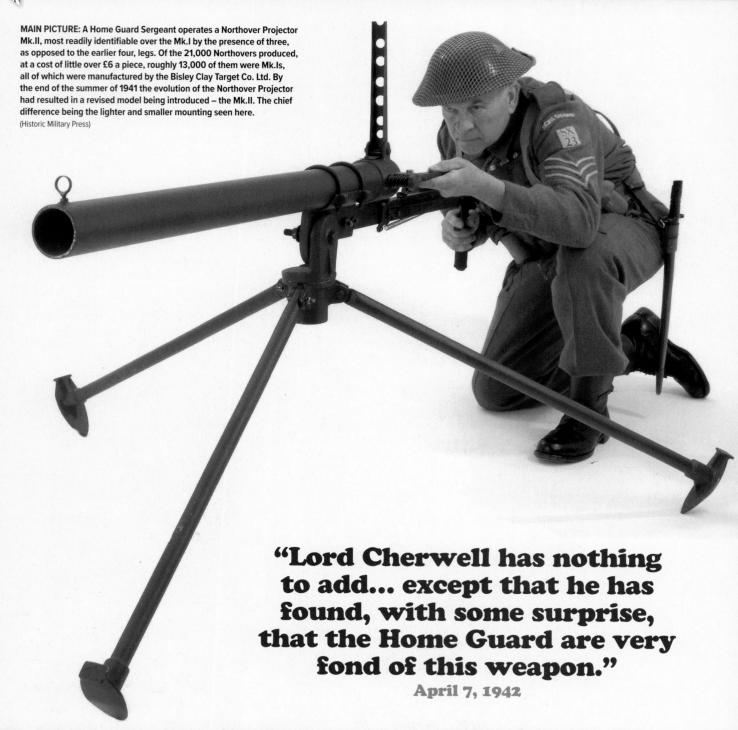

MAIN PICTURE: A Home Guard Sergeant operates a Northover Projector Mk.II, most readily identifiable over the Mk.I by the presence of three, as opposed to the earlier four, legs. Of the 21,000 Northovers produced, at a cost of little over £6 a piece, roughly 13,000 of them were Mk.Is, all of which were manufactured by the Bisley Clay Target Co. Ltd. By the end of the summer of 1941 the evolution of the Northover Projector had resulted in a revised model being introduced – the Mk.II. The chief difference being the lighter and smaller mounting seen here.
(Historic Military Press)

"Lord Cherwell has nothing to add… except that he has found, with some surprise, that the Home Guard are very fond of this weapon."

April 7, 1942

WEAPONS OF THE HOME GUARD:
Northover Projector

T he Northover Projector was a smooth-bore, breech-loading weapon that had been intended to be used in an anti-tank role. Incredibly basic in design, the Northover would be the first weapon in the sub-artillery class to be made available to the Home Guard, a move that, in reality, may have been of greater value psychologically than in practical terms.

Initially called the Northover (Bottle) Mortar, the projector was named after its inventor Major H R Northover OBE, MC, a retired army officer and a Director of the Bisley Clay Target Company. No stranger to the subject of weapon design, having been involved in such work in the First World, Northover, serving in his village's LDV unit, was acutely aware of the shortage of weapons and he promptly set about designing a weapon that could project Molotov Cocktails.

Northover worked on developing his project throughout May 1940, all of which effort was undertaken at his own expense. By the end of May, and at the request of Churchill himself, Northover took his first prototype to Downing Street. Having now seen the projector, Churchill instructed that it be taken to Hangmoor Range, near Aldershot, for firing trials.

The tests duly took place on July 28, 1940, with the Northover firing the A.W. phosphorous bomb – subsequently, as we have seen, known as the SIP Grenade or No.76 Grenade. This summary was prepared for Churchill two days later: "Two A.W. bombs were projected at a light tank approaching the firer. The first went over the tank at about 120 yards range, whereas the second hit the visor of the tank and flame actually entered the tank causing the driver to evacuate as quickly as possible. There is certainly value in this mortar – particularly against open vehicles, aeroplanes on landing, etc and it is proposed to put it into production as soon as possible." No sooner had this statement been made, then production of the Mk.I began.

The 10th Wiltshire (Pewsey) Battalion received its first issue of Northovers on September 7, 1941. The battalion history includes the following reflections: "We received the first of these much-maligned drainpipes to-day, but we think that they are quite useful weapons. They were issued originally for throwing grenades. Sometimes they did, and sometimes they did not, and not infrequently the bottle of phosphorous burst in the barrel with a flammenwerfer effect, but seldom would they burst on impact as the ground was too soft."

Major-General W J Eldridge, Director General of Armaments, gave the following assessment of the Northover in November 1948: "To assess this invention at its true value, one should, I think, cast their mind back to the state of affairs after Dunkirk in 1940. The Home Guard was just forming and there were no weapons available for them. The best that could be produced was the Molotov Cocktail, hand thrown. Mr. Northover's projector did at least increase the range of the Molotov from 25 to 200 yards... Another point which has to be borne in mind is that, although the Northover Projector was not used in action, its value might have been very great had the Germans invaded Great Britain, as seemed highly probable in the days before the end of the Battle of Britain... Was this of military value? I think the answer can only be 'yes'."

Perhaps this was the crux of the matter. For, if nothing else, the Northover Projector was, for all its limitations, faults and Heath Robinson appearance, at least something, in a complete dearth of anything more suitable, with which the Home Guard of 1940 and 1941 could fight an invasion.

ABOVE: Members of a Home Guard unit being trained in the operation and firing of the Northover Projector. (Historic Military Press)

MANUAL OF THE NORTHOVER PROJECTOR

AND K.W. REVOLVER-PROJECTOR

Components
Stripping
Assembling

Care and Maintenance
Ammunition
Tactical Handling

1/6

With Introduction to the Sten Machine Carbine

ABOVE: A commercially-published manual for the Northover Projector. (Historic Military Press)

ABOVE: Another view of a Northover Projector Mk.II. (Historic Military Press)

ABOVE: Volunteers from the Palace of Westminster Home Guard pictured being instructed on a wheeled Northover Projector during March 1942. (Historic Military Press)

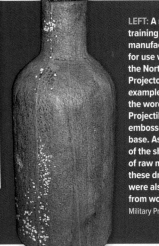

LEFT: A rubber training round manufactured for use with the Northover Projector. This example has the words 'Drill Projectile' embossed on the base. As a reult of the shortage of raw materials, these drill rounds were also made from wood. (Historic Military Press)

An American Legion

Among the many unusual or specialist units formed under the auspices of the Home Guard was one whose ranks were filled only by, and funded through, American citizens.

Winston Churchill and General Wade Hayes, commander of the 1st American Motorized Squadron, examine one of the unit's armoured cars. The original caption points out that the vehicle was "built on an American chassis and equipped with items such as a periscope (see the left-hand side of the windscreen panel) and sealed door; it is almost certain this vehicle was possibly imported complete from the United States".
(Historic Military Press)

In an editorial on September 13, 1940, the *Market Harborough Advertiser and Midland Mail* briefly reported on what it called "one of the most impressive signs of American co-operation in the war". This was, the paper noted, "to be found in Buckingham Gate", London.

"This is the headquarters of what many there like to call America's Legion," the paper continued. "The inspiring figure of the effort is Mr. A. P. Buquor, famous as an inventor of mobile equipment for the forces. As soon as the United States department of Justice ruled that Americans on British soil could enlist, he set to work to raise the Legion. He met with striking success.

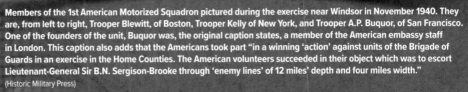

Members of the 1st American Motorized Squadron pictured during the exercise near Windsor in November 1940. They are, from left to right, Trooper Blewitt, of Boston, Trooper Kelly of New York, and Trooper A.P. Buquor, of San Francisco. One of the founders of the unit, Buquor was, the original caption states, a member of the American embassy staff in London. This caption also adds that the Americans took part "in a winning 'action' against units of the Brigade of Guards in an exercise in the Home Counties. The American volunteers succeeded in their object which was to escort Lieutenant-General Sir B.N. Sergison-Brooke through 'enemy lines' of 12 miles' depth and four miles width."
(Historic Military Press)

"The Americans have formed units armed at their own expense with fast cars, light machine guns, Tommy guns, Mills bombs and other weapons. Mr. Buquor's first recruit was Charles Sweeney, the famous golfer, and it was said that he has since done some very successful recruiting. Brigadier-General Wade H. Hayes, who was on General Pershing's staff, is in command. The intention is that this Legion shall form a special mobile reserve which can go to any point in the defence system when the need arises.'

Authorised by a Special Order in Council signed by King George VI in September 1940, and officially known as the 1st American Motorized Squadron Home Guard, but also referred to as the American Troop or the American Squadron, the unit's formation was met with disapproval by the then American ambassador, Joseph Kennedy Sr. Believing that Britain would fall to Hitler's forces, Kennedy was concerned that the unit's existence could, in the event of a German invasion, lead to US citizens living in London being shot as *francs-tireurs*. This situation improved following Kennedy's resignation on October 22, 1940. His replacement, John G. Winant, proved far more sympathetic towards the unit and its activities.

One of the squadron's earliest members was Charles G. Tubbs, who, with a long-standing background in advertising and publicity, also edited its inhouse newsletter, *Yankee Yahoo*, the first edition of which was published on 30 August 1940. Of his

service with the unit, Tubbs once declared: "I live to fight Germans and Japs, and the Italians if I happen to think of them. Nobody pays me to fight these chaps, so I do it for philanthropic reasons and earn a living in occasional spare time. I fight the Germans every Tuesday and Thursday from 5.30 to 7 p.m. and every Saturday from noon until God knows when. I do this by going to 58 Buckingham Gate."

SUBHEADING

It was not just at its headquarters that the men of the 1st American Squadron undertook their training. Indeed, an account of an exercise which took place near Windsor was published in the *Falkirk Herald* on November 13, 1940: "The first motorised squadron of the Home Guard formed by Americans living in London held their exercises in the Home Counties on Sunday [November 10]. They have been receiving technical instruction from officers of the Brigade of Guards, and these officers were umpires at the manoeuvres. The 'enemy' had occupied a line and were moving forward to the north, and the American Squadron stood between them and further advancement. It was also the Home Guards' duty to see that a British General who had escaped 'capture' reached safety. This was accomplished by holding up the invaders with barbed wire and smoke bombs, and by getting the General away in a strange car, without his hat and with a girl as his companion." »

In a similar vein, it is known that the unit attended a training course at Pirbright Camp in Surrey early in 1941. This was referred to by one participant as the squadron's "third period of training".

On January 9, 1941, Winston Churchill, as part of his effort to influence American public opinion in support of the British war effort, reviewed the squadron during a special parade held on Horse Guards Parade in London. "He was accompanied by Mrs Churchill and by Lieutenant-General Sir Bertram Sergison-Brooke, General Officer Commanding, London District," noted *The Times* the next day. "About 50 members of the squadron – out of a total strength of 72 – were on parade, wearing the familiar khaki uniform and armlet of the Home Guard. Each man also wore a red eagle badge on his arm just below the shoulder and was equipped with a Winchester automatic rifle. Behind the ranks of the squadron were its motor-cars, each a high-powered American vehicle voluntarily presented for service. At the end of the line was a dispatch rider with motor-cycle.

"Brigadier-General Wade H. Hayes, a veteran of the Spanish-American War and commander of this American squadron of the Home Guard, accompanied Mr Churchill as he passed along the squadron's ranks and shook hands with each of the troop leaders. The Prime Minister, at the end of his brief review, complimented the squadron on its smart appearance and expressed his appreciation of this voluntary participation by American citizens in the defence of Britain."

In its coverage of the parade, *The Times* also provided an interesting insight into the unit's formation and operation: "The 1st American Motorized Squadron of the Home Guard began its official existence last September, when the appropriate Order in Council sanctioning its formation was signed. The squadron had, however, had an unofficial existence for some months before that and had attracted to its ranks a fair proportion of those American citizens whose work and other interests keep them in London in spite of the war.

"Today it is attached to the headquarters of the London District, and, in the picturesque phrase of its commander, its members are regarded as the household troops of General Sergison-Brooke, for whom they provide security. The squadron trains three nights a week at the former headquarters in Westminster of a Territorial Army unit, and on Saturdays it practises at the rifle ranges outside London. On occasional Sundays a 'scheme' is carried out in the country. In each of these branches of training the squadron has been assisted by instructors from the Brigade of Guards.

"The squadron is, of course, made up entirely of American citizens. Many people who, according to General Hayes, can be described only technically as American citizens have attempted to enrol in the squadron but have been rejected. The men now on the roll are described by General Hayes as an astonishing cross-section of the people for so small a group. They include engineers, lawyers, clerks, doctors, and newspaper men. Many of them, like their commander, served in Europe with the U.S.A. Army during the last War.

ABOVE: Men of the 1st American Motorized Squadron during an exercise. The original caption states: "Last week in maneuvers [sic] they gave the British Army a rude shock. Using Fifth Columnists who played golf, walked dogs, pretended to be drunk, the Americans scouted out, surrounded and captured the headquarters of a crack British brigade." (Historic Military Press)

"A consignment of the newest type of Thompson automatic machine-guns has been sent from America."

ABOVE: Winston Churchill inspecting the ranks of the 1st American Motorized Squadron on Horse Guards Parade, January 9, 1941. (via Historic Military Press)

ABOVE: Winston Churchill salutes members of the 1st American Motorized Squadron, Home Guard during the parade held on Horse Guards Parade in London on January 9, 1941. (via Historic Military Press)

"The squadron's motor-cars have been presented to it by its own members in most cases. A consignment of the newest type of Thompson automatic machine-guns has been sent from America." The Thompson submachine-guns referred to here were obtained through the efforts of Charles Sweeney, who, utilising his contacts in the United States, persuaded the Thompson Company to contribute 100 submachine-guns and 100,000 rounds of ammunition. It is also worth pointing out that contemporary sources state that the squadron took on the responsibility of guarding the London District HQ one night in eight.

During a recruitment drive in the summer of 1941, Hayes penned a letter to *The Times*, which was duly published on August 6: "In recent weeks so many of the younger members of the First American Squadron of the Home Guard have joined the British Army, the Royal Navy, the Royal Air Force, the Fleet Air Arm, and the Transatlantic Ferry Pilot Service that the unit is now below its maximum strength. We are anxious to maintain the efficiency of the squadron by filling the vacancies which are being created for so excellent a purpose... We were obliged at one time to refuse further applications for membership as our personnel must be limited. This is due to the fact that the unit is motorized and has been assigned a highly specialized operational role. Now that vacancies are available, I am confident that our fellow countrymen here will respond in the same spirit which brought the American Squadron into existence in London a little more than a year ago.

"This service can be undertaken by any man of middle age who is in normal physical condition, and it will not interfere with business except in the event of invasion. Members take no oath of allegiance and

their American citizenship is not affected. The squadron has been fully equipped with arms and vehicles given by American friends and it is trained thoroughly for special service under the guidance of officers and non-commissioned officers of the Brigade of Guards. Membership involves no personal expense, although we have commodious quarters which include a drill hall, a rifle range, and clubrooms.'

Despite changes in personnel, the unit retained its presence in London throughout the months and years that followed. On Sunday, October 24, 1943, for example, the American Home Guards participated in a wide-ranging exercise held in London, a detailed account of which was published in *The Times* the following morning: "All Home Guard and Civil Defence units in the London District took part yesterday in the biggest-scale exercise that has taken

place in London. They were called out in the early morning to deal with 'airborne invaders' who attacked at more than 100 scattered points. 'Thunder' flashes and blank cartridges resounded in the quiet streets as the 'battle' was fought with great vigour... The object of the exercise was to test the defence scheme for London, and he could say definitely that he was very pleased with the result. The exercise had shown that the defence scheme did work in practice. He paid tribute to the cooperation of the civil defence and the police.

"As a whole the enemy attacks, launched by a determined force of the Regular Army, failed. Surprise helped the 'enemy' to gain initial advantages and capture certain important points, but in practically every case they were turned out before the cease fire. A high percentage of the Home Guard turned out, a muster which staff officers considered excellent, and as proving that there has been a great improvement in communications and mobility. At a number of vital factories the attackers were dealt with easily by the factory Home Guard. At an R.A.F. station where the 'enemy' obtained a footing, men of the R.A.F. Regiment, again with the Home Guard, put in a counter-attack and dislodged them quickly.

"One party of the enemy captured some motor-boats on the Thames and made a water-borne landing with sore success. Naval units, certain R.A.F. sections, and the whole of the A.A. defences collaborated. Sixty loud-speaker vans from the Ministry of Information helped in the call out, touring districts with audible orders for the Home Guard to assemble...

"General Smith was at his headquarters when, soon after 7 a.m., a strong party of the 'enemy' delivered a heavy attack. The American Squadron of the Home Guard defended London District Headquarters, and they carried out their task so well that the umpires ruled that the 'enemy' had been beaten off.

ABOVE: The United States' Ambassador to Great Britain, the Hon. J.G. Winant, is pictured inspecting American and Canadian Home Guard volunteers, all members of the 1st American Motorized Squadron, at Wellington Barracks, London, on July 4, 1942. (Department of National Defence/Library and Archives Canada) INSET: The badge issued to members of the American Troop Home Guard, also known as the American Mechanised Defence Corps or the 1st American Motorized Squadron. (Richard Hunt Collection)

Churchill's Secret Army

Whilst the Home Guard was created to help combat a German invasion, there was a part of the organisation which, whilst legally an integral part of the Home Guard, answered directly to GHQ Home Forces. Known as the Auxiliary Units, this secretive body of men was to swing into action only after an enemy landing.

BELOW: Located beside Furzebrook Road in the village of East Creech in Dorset, this memorial commemorates the seven men who formed the local Home Guard Auxiliary Unit. The unit's Operational Base is located to the east of the memorial at the lower slopes of Knowle Hill – in the background in this image.

(Historic Military Press)

THE
CREECH BARROW
SEVEN
AUXILIARY UNIT
G.H.Q. HOME FORCES

1940 - 1944

Sgt. FRED SIMPSON
Cpl. DOUG GREEN
Pte. LES GREEN
Pte. HAROLD HATCHARD
Pte. JACK HATCHARD
Pte. ELI KITCATT
Pte. WILF STOCKLEY

MAY THEY REST IN PEACE
IN THE LAND THEY WERE
PREPARED TO DEFEND
WHEN IT WAS IN
MORTAL DANGER

It all began, like so many initiatives during the war, with Winston Churchill. On June 29, 1940, the Secretary of State for War, Anthony Eden, visited XII Corps, which was responsible for the entire coastal strip from Greenwich to Hayling Island. He was shocked at discovering the weakness of the defences of what was the most likely area to be targeted by the Germans in the event of invasion. Eden expressed his concerns to the prime minister, and, fully appreciative of the perilous situation the country was in following the evacuation from Dunkirk, Churchill invited the commander of XII Corps, Lieutenant General Andrew Thorne, to Chequers for lunch the following day.

Although no detailed record of the lunch at Chequers was kept, there was agreement that the forces available would have considerable difficulty in stopping the invaders should they succeed in

ABOVE: Easy to miss, this is the entrance to a rural Operational Base. (Courtesy of Arthur Ward)

ABOVE: Escape tunnel exits on the Operational Bases were as carefully disguised as the main entrances. This one emerges in a river bank some distance from an Operational Base in East Sussex. (Courtesy of Arthur Ward)

landing. Following the meeting, Churchill instructed General Ismay, the Prime Minister's representative on the Chiefs of Staff Committee, to evaluate the practicality of 'drenching' the invasion beaches with mustard gas. Though this somewhat extreme option was not adopted, that lunch at Chequers was to have even more far-reaching effects, for it revived an idea that General Thorne had first considered years before – the formation of a 'stay behind' guerrilla resistance force in Britain. After the meeting with Churchill, Thorne got in touch with General Ismay, raising his idea for a covert resistance force which, in the event of invasion, would operate behind enemy lines.

Ismay was receptive to the idea and he proposed that a young officer who worked within military intelligence should come and see him to discuss matters further. The officer Ismay had in mind was none other

ABOVE & INSET: Some Operational Bases, like this one beneath The Tottington Manor Hotel in Sussex, were actually concealed beneath existing buildings. Here an 'Auxiliary' descends beneath the floor of the hotel's wine cellar to enter the hideout below. (Courtesy of Arthur Ward)

than Peter Fleming, the traveller, author, special correspondent for *The Times* and brother of James Bond's creator, Ian Fleming. Peter Fleming worked for M.I.(R) (Military Intelligence (Research)), a semi-secret department within the War Office.

In 1939 Fleming had written *Notes on the Possibilities of British Military Action in China* for M.I.(R), into which he and others had been covertly recruited in 1938. M.I.(R) considered Fleming to be the best candidate to establish a British guerrilla unit, a force that would be comprised of men who could live off the land. So, in a secluded farmhouse called the Garth in Bilting, Kent, Fleming set up the first regional training centre for a new, British, stay-behind force. This, the first Auxiliary Unit, was known by the cover name 'XII Corps Observation Unit'.

RECRUITING THE AUXILIARIES

The man chosen to head up the new organisation was Colonel Colin Gubbins, who had considerable experience and expertise in guerrilla warfare and had led the Independent Companies, the predecessors of the British Commandos, in the recent failed Norway campaign. The name given to the new organisation was that of the Home Guard Auxiliaries, it being thought that such a nondescript term was unlikely to arouse unnecessary attention – and secrecy was fundamental to the entire concept.

After the first unit had been formed in Kent, the second most likely invasion area was East Anglia, and it was there that Captain Andrew Croft was invited to set up a similar organisation. In Sussex, Captain ➤➤

ABOVE & INSET: If they had to leave quickly or in an emergency, Auxiliaries did not exit the way they entered – they used concealed lengths of escape tunnel (usually constructed from lengths of pre-cast concrete piping) to affect their escape. Here, an Auxiliary can be seen peering down the 100m escape tunnel at Tottington Manor. (Courtesy of Arthur Ward)

John Gwynn, the owner of extensive swathes of land around Lewes and Arundel, was asked to do likewise, as were other individuals across the country. Such was the rapid rate of progress that by August 15, 1940, the first phase of recruitment had been completed; the basic organisation was in place, men were being trained, and stores had been delivered. A total of 2,300 men had been recruited and organised into 350 patrols of around six to eight men each.

There was, however, little confidence in their effectiveness at this stage. A progress report issued at the time stated: "Whereas all the men recruited were determined to do their utmost to harass the enemy's rear and lines of communication, it was, in fact, doubtful whether many of them would have been able to survive the first few days of invasion." In fact, life expectancy once the Auxiliaries become operational in the event of an invasion was estimated at just twelve days. Nevertheless, by the end of August, the Auxiliary Unit organisation stretched as far north as Brechin on Scotland's east coast, south to Land's End and north of the Bristol Channel as far as Pembroke Dock.

Recruits to the Auxiliaries were mostly drawn from the ranks of the Home Guard, often men in reserved occupations who had joined up immediately when they heard Eden's call for volunteers to form the LDV. Such men were clearly highly patriotic. Rather than the more elderly recruits of the Home Guard who were too old to join the regular forces, the men in the reserved occupation tended to be younger and more physically capable. The recruits were issued with Home Guard uniforms carrying the unit insignia of one of three battalions that had been established to provide cover for the whole nation. These were 201 Battalion, which covered Scotland and the northern counties of England, 202 Battalion, located

THE ORIGINAL HIDE-OUT

ABOVE: To this day the original model and pattern for the perfect Operational Base still exists in the grounds of Coleshill Estate, in a thicket a little distance from where the house itself (destroyed in a fire in 1952) once stood. The only major difference from Operational Bases in the field is where there would normally have been an entrance to the escape tunnel, there is a large walk-in entrance instead. This was presumably fashioned to allow plenty of room for students to observe the entire living chamber without having to resort to commando techniques every time they chose to enter it. This Operational Base also benefits from the addition of substantial concrete re-enforcements, a luxury that certainly wouldn't have been the norm in 1940. An interesting detail which still survives is the vertical chimney-flue exit, which passed through a dummy tree trunk that had been cemented in place above the roof. (Courtesy of Gaius Cornelius)

ABOVE: The old Post Office in Coleshill, this being the building to which Auxiliaries were ordered to arrive for their training courses at nearby Coleshill House. A plaque commemorating this fact can be seen on the wall. (Courtesy of Michael Gibb, www.geograph.org.uk)

in the Midlands, and 203 Battalion, which was in London and the southern counties. In addition to the Home Guard, the Auxiliaries were stiffened by more than 100 regular Army officers and 600 other ranks who volunteered to join this special force.

By wearing uniforms, it was hoped that if captured by the enemy within their lines or rear areas, they would not be shot as spies but treated as prisoners of war. This was perhaps a vain wish, as Hitler had decreed that all members of the Home Guard should be considered civilian subversives and were to be shot regardless. The Auxiliaries knew these risks, and fully understood that, if captured they were likely to be tortured to reveal their hideouts and the other members of their unit, and then shot.

Rather than endure such treatment, the men might have to consider shooting themselves if faced with unavoidable capture.

SCOUT PATROLS
The Auxiliaries role was defined in a letter sent to Churchill, by Duncan Sandys at the War Cabinet, on August 8, 1940. They were to operate in small bodies which would, "act offensively on the flanks and rear of any enemy troops who may obtain a foothold in this country. Their action will particularly be directed against tanks and lorries in lagger [actually laager, meaning an encampment protected by a circle of wagons or armoured vehicles], ammunition dumps, small enemy posts and stragglers."[1] The Auxiliaries were

also expected to snipe at the enemy where possible. The other function of the Auxiliaries was to provide a system of intelligence which would be fed to the regular forces to keep them informed of what was happening behind the enemy's front line.

These small bodies were to consist, for the most part, of not more than a dozen men under a selected leader. As it was anticipated that their subversive activities would generally occur under the cover of darkness, it was essential that the members of each party should have a very good knowledge of the countryside in which they would operate; for that reason, many of the recruits in the rural areas were men who worked on the land. It was expected, therefore, that many of the recruits would be farmers, gamekeepers and their old adversaries, poachers. They were to operate in 'Scout Patrols' of a leader and no more than four men. Patrols were only to be conducted if the result was worth risking the lives of the men in the patrol. Combat was to be avoided unless the odds were considerably in the patrol's favour. Rather, the patrols were to be used to attack undefended supply lorries if that was possible. They could potentially attack convoys, providing there were no infantry escorts. If there were accompanying enemy infantry, a roadblock was to be employed, which would be put in place after the escort had passed.

With so much equipment having been abandoned by the Army during the retreat to Dunkirk, it was far from easy at first to arm the Auxiliaries with all the weapons that it would have been desirable. It was hoped that they could be armed with rifles, grenades and a variety of explosive devices, including delayed-action fuzes, plastic explosives and incendiary bombs, as well as Thompson sub-machineguns when they were available. In reality, many Auxiliaries brought with them

their own shotguns, for which they were issued single-ball cartridges, their grenades being Molotov cocktails. Home-made weapons for close combat ranged from their own long-since-used Boy Scout knives, to knuckledusters and over-the-counter daggers. They made their own garrotting wires and 'thrust' weapons in the form of T-shaped carpenter's bradawls as well as fashioning their own wooden clubs. The men were also issued with rubber truncheons intended for riot control in some distant part of the empire, which had been found in War Department warehouses. Churchill had insisted that the Auxiliaries were issued with revolvers, but this was more easily ordered than achieved. Colt .32 automatics were brought in from America and in one early deal revolvers, ammunition, belts and holsters were sent from the New York Police Department.[2]

Over time, these makeshift measures were replaced, or in many cases added to, with more standard weapons, including Sten guns. However, firearms were considered to be weapons of last resort. With the Auxiliaries operating mainly at night, the bang and flash from the discharge of any gun would instantly reveal their whereabouts.

To partially overcome this, a semi-silenced gun fitted luminous sights, the Welrod, was recommended for the Auxiliaries. Also used by the likes of the Special Operations Executive, the Welrod was a single-shot, bolt-action handgun, the muzzle end of which was ground slightly concave to minimise noise during firing. It had a low muzzle-velocity and was only effective at close quarters.

AN UNDERGROUND EXISTENCE

The Auxiliaries' underground hideouts, or 'Operational Bases', were situated in the most inaccessible locations, or those that enemy »

ABOVE: A reconstruction of the equipment that may have been worn by the average Home Guard Auxiliary. In this case, the 'volunteer' has been issued with the latest variation of wartime battledress – the 1940 Utility Pattern. He is wearing a 1937 Pattern webbing waist belt and anklets and has been issued with a sniper's camouflage printed face veil. Well-armed, he is carrying a .45 calibre Thompson sub-machinegun, his Fairbairn Sykes fighting knife and a Smith & Wesson .38 revolver in the holster. On this occasion he is not wearing the rubber boots that came to be issued. The latter were useful for two reasons. Firstly, because of the rubber tongue which sealed the boot, they were waterproof (essential for so much outdoor work in the woods, etc.) and, secondly, because, as one Auxiliary recalled, "they were good for creeping around in quietly". (Courtesy of Richard Hunt)

ABOVE: An example of the Welrod Mk.I pistol. This 9mm weapon was intended primarily for use by uniformed Special Forces personnel. (Historic Military Press)

LEFT: A set of knuckle-dusters, such as those that many members of the Auxiliary Units recalled carrying. (Historic Military Press)

"We learnt detailed info about where to stick a knife in."

ABOVE: Many of the Operational Bases have not survived the passage of time, as this example in woodland near the West Sussex village of Wiston shows. The main chamber has completely collapsed. (Historic Military Press)

troops would be unlikely or unprepared to investigate too closely. Suitable locations included excavations within muddy riverbanks or deep within inaccessible bramble-strewn woods. As well as some of the patrol's weapons, each Operational Base was fitted out with bedding, lighting and heating, and stocked with several weeks' supply of food (in the form of ration packs) and water. The actual inventory for a typical Operational Base included: "Holsters, groundsheets, blankets, rubber boots (agricultural type), water bottles, carriers and slings – one for each man; a wire cutter, monocular and case, a Tilley lamp, two Primus stoves, and one Elsan chemical closet. One pair of telephones with half a mile of cable, a first aid kit (with morphia), water sterilisation sets and three shell dressings."

The first aid equipment included a gallon jar of rum for emergency purposes only, to relieve pain in the event of injury, or in the face of imminent capture. Smoking inside the Operational Bases was restricted to ten minutes in every hour.

The Operational Bases were usually constructed either by teams of Royal Engineers or miners brought in from outside the area so that they could not reveal the locations of the hideouts to anyone in the locality, or by the patrols themselves. It is said that when the Operational Bases were built by outside labour, upon completion and the place was to be handed over to the patrol, the Auxiliaries were challenged to find their way into the hideout. None were able to do so until shown how.[3] Some indication of how well concealed the Operational Bases were can be gleaned

from an incident involving the Cooksbridge patrol in Sussex. One morning, after being in their hideout overnight, they cooked themselves bacon and eggs for breakfast. The smell of the cooking food drifted into the nostrils of someone walking by. The individual could smell the food but could not see where it was coming from, which made him very suspicious and he reported it to the police.[4]

In August 1940, it was decided that the Auxiliaries needed a centralised training facility to ensure the patrols were fully conversant with every element of their roles. This was formed at Coleshill House at Highworth, near Swindon, which was set in its own extensive grounds far from prying eyes. Such was the degree of security set up around Coleshill House, trainees were not sent directly to the house but instead were instructed to report to Highworth Post Office. When they arrived at the Post Office, the Postmistress, Mabel Stranks, would telephone Coleshill House and tell them that there was a parcel waiting to be picked up. A vehicle would then be sent, and the identity of the trainee verified before being taken to the house.

ABOVE: The majority of Operational Bases were little more than Nissen Huts sunk deep beneath the surface. This well-preserved example, pictured with much of the interior fittings still present., was used by the Staplefield patrol and is located in woodland west of Haywards Heath in Sussex. The open door leads to the entrance shaft. (Courtesy of Arthur Ward)

Patrol leaders (and later some ordinary patrol members) attended weekend courses at the school. Training covered the weapons and equipment that the patrols were expected to use. Subjects such as giving effective orders and map reading were also covered. Once the leaders returned to their patrols, they trained the members of their patrol.

'WHERE TO STICK A KNIFE IN'

One member of an Auxiliary patrol in Devon, Geoffrey Bradford, recalled his training experiences: "Coleshill mainly consisted of lectures, principally in unarmed combat based on W.E. Fairbairn's book [and knife]... We learnt detailed information about where to stick a knife in. The idea was that you used it from behind. It was a stabbing knife – the blade wasn't all that sharp. You wouldn't take anyone on from the front but hold them around the neck and in up through the ribs. It takes quite a

ABOVE: Seen here with a fighting knife, *The Countryman's Diary* was the Auxiliary Units' cunningly disguised handbook of mayhem. Its pages revealed the best way to ambush an enemy patrol, demolish a supply dump or set booby traps using the state-of-the-art time pencils and plastic explosives members of Auxiliary Units were given in priority over regular British Army units – much to the fury of many on the army staff! (Courtesy of Arthur Ward)

ABOVE: A reconstruction of how the interior of an Operational Base might have appeared during the war. It was unveiled in 2004 at the Museum of the British Resistance Organisation at Parham in Suffolk. (Courtesy of Gaius Cornelius)

ABOVE: The late Frank Penfold, leader of an Auxiliary Unit patrol which operated in the countryside near Arundel in West Sussex, reluctantly brandishes his surviving fighting knife. Like many other Auxiliaries, Frank wrapped the weapon's metal grip with insulating tape in order to secure a firmer hold should it be covered in blood. (Courtesy of Arthur Ward)

ABOVE: Fixed to a trig point on the North Devon coast near Woolacombe is a memorial plaque that commemorates those members of the Auxiliary Units' 203 Battalion that served in the surrounding area.

(Simon J. Beer/Shutterstock)

time to die from a knife if you can't get it into the heart. You would have to stab them enough times and hang on there to see what happened. We also learned how to use the 'garrotte', which was better than the dagger for throat-cutting. Rubber truncheons and coshes – some were individually made, of pre-war origin – were also used. Cheese-wires fitted to two simple toggles were popular."[5]

In Kent, one of the more probable landing areas because of its long range of flat open beaches, there were thirty (or possibly thirty-three) separate Auxiliary Units. They functioned entirely independently from each other, carrying out their normal civilian jobs, but training in complete secrecy. The patrols operated from several Operational Bases, most of which had been sited and designed by Peter Fleming. In total, twenty-eight such hideouts were constructed, ranging from a two-man post under an old sheep trough in Charing Hill to the north-west of Ashford, to a large hideout that could accommodate 120 people which had been built in an old airship launching pit in King's Wood, Challock, due north of Ashford. The entrance to the King's Wood Operational Base was concealed with a large tree trunk which weighed half a ton. It was moved by a counter-balance and was so cleverly built that when it was touched in the correct place, would swing back to expose the entrance.[6] Each Operational Base would normally also have an emergency exit.

As an indication of the scale of the Auxiliaries, Sussex had twenty-three (or possibly twenty-four) patrols with a total of 139 Auxiliaries, making an average of around six men per patrol. Hampshire, meanwhile, had forty-seven patrols, the highest number in the country, with 301 men, making an average of approximately seven per patrol.[7]

The Auxiliary Units very quickly became quite proficient and, after the rather

bleak assessment given in mid-August, by early September 1940, the units were considered much more effective, most with their own Operational Bases already constructed and their men trained. They had also undertaken a 'good' number of exercises at night, including some which involved the Regular Army. A report at that date, declared that: "A high proportion may confidently be expected to remain in security behind the enemy lines for a considerable period. Their night training coupled with their local knowledge, should give them an undisputed advantage over any enemy troops in their area."[8]

Of course, the Auxiliary Units were never called into action and the force was disbanded in January 1945, having been initially stood down in November the previous year. After the war, those members of the Home Guard who served for at least three years were eligible to receive the Defence Medal. Despite the dangerous work they were to undertake in the event of an invasion, the Honours Committee decided that members of the Auxiliary Units – men who had volunteered knowing full well that their chances of survival in the event of an invasion would be counted in days – were not eligible for the medal.

NOTES

1. Quoted in Stewart Angell, *The Secret Sussex Resistance 1940-1944* (Middleton Press, Midhurst, 1996), pp.9-10.
2. John Warwicker, *Churchill's Underground Army, A History of the Auxiliary Units in World War II* (Frontline, Barnsley, 2008), pp.126-7.
3. K.R. Gulvin, *Kent Home Guard, A History* (North Kent Books, Rainham, 1980), p.86.
4. Stewart Angell, ibid, p.29.
5. Quoted in Arthur Ward, *Resisting the Nazi Invader* (Constable, London, 1997), p.49.
6. K.R. Gulvin, ibid, p.85.
7. Stewart Angell, ibid, p.24.
8. See russellphillips.uk/home-guard-auxiliary-units.

Dedicated to the Volunteers of the 203 DEVON British Resistance Movement known as "AUXILIARY UNITS" of this area 1940 - 1944

"It rapidly became popular, and it was found to be a very accurate weapon that could be relied on."

An official history of the 10th Wiltshire (Pewsey) Battalion

MAIN PICTURE: A Blacker Bombard, also officially known as the 29mm Spigot Mortar, ready for firing by a Home Guard Sergeant.
(Historic Military Press)

WEAPONS OF THE HOME GUARD:
Blacker Bombard

Even before the outbreak of war, Lieutenant-Colonel L V S Blacker had begun exploring how best to utilise the concept of the spigot mortar. As 1939 drifted into 1940, he enlisted the help of a local clockmaker and between the two of them the first prototype of the Blacker Bombard was completed.

Through sheer persistence, Blacker then managed to bring his design to the attention of Major Millis Jefferis, who was in charge of a rather unorthodox War Office department known simply as M.D.1 (for Ministry of Defence 1), this being a small group of officers and scientists tasked with devising special weapons for irregular warfare. Impressed by what he saw, Jefferis ordered that further development be undertaken.

The turning point came on August 18, 1940. That day the mortar was demonstrated to Winston Churchill at Chequers. After an operator error, which unleashed a round that nearly hit one of the witnesses, no less a personage than General de Gaulle, a re-run saw the target successfully hit. The Prime Minister immediately turned to Jefferis: "I instruct you to proceed with all speed with the development of this excellent weapon."

Perhaps concerned at the pace of this work, on March 26, 1941, Churchill wrote to M.D.1. He urged that they, "must make, or get made, a first batch of 2,500 spigot mortars, complete with ammunition, as soon as possible". Then, on April 29, Field Marshal Lord Alanbrooke attended a further demonstration of the Blacker Bombard on the ranges at Bisley. A few days later he issued instructions that some 12,000 of the mortars should "be manufactured with all haste".

By September 21, 1941, the first supplies of the Blacker Bombard must have arrived, for on that day Churchill noted that "many bombards are now being delivered". By the end of January 1942, some 6,500 had been issued. As 1943 dawned, production was all but complete, so much so that the Home Guard units had 18,691 Blacker Bombards in their hands.

In service, the Blacker Bombard was met with mixed reactions. A report produced by Southern Command on November 3, 1941 stated: "We tried the weapon with a trained crew against both stationary targets and targets representing moving tanks at both 300 and 500 yards range. No direct hits were scored in a large number of rounds fired. Even at 200 yards, the trajectory is unlikely to be sufficiently flat to produce accurate shooting." The report's author, the Brigade Commander of the Salisbury Plain Area, concluded with a final, terse petition: "From the national point of view, I sincerely hope that further production of this ineffective weapon has been stopped."

A similarly disgruntled General Sir George Herbert, the Commanding Officer of the 3rd Wiltshire (Warminster) Battalion, felt compelled to forward his opinions to the War Office: "I understand that this weapon is to be forced on the Home Guard, and I therefore wish to protest as strongly as I can at this waste of public money on a useless and out-of-date weapon."

A different perspective is provided by one Colonel Pollock, an instructor at No.1 Home Guard School at Dorking, Surrey, in May 1941: "This is the most impressive weapon demonstrated at the school. It is very accurate indeed… It is an extremely useful weapon".

Whatever its faults and problems, perceived or real, the Blacker Bombard still afforded the Home Guard, when there was little to replace it, with the means of taking the fight to the enemy. For a large part of the Home Guard's existence, the Blacker Bombard would provide its best, if not only, anti-tank capability.

ABOVE: A re-enactment of a Blacker Bombard pictured mounted on a surviving concrete pedestal mount. (Historic Military Press)

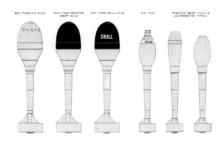

ABOVE: An original wartime diagram detailing the various types of live and drill, or training, bombs for use with the Blacker Bombard. (Historic Military Press)

RIGHT: A set of training notes for the Blacker Bombard that were issued for Staffordshire Home Guard battalions by the Weapon Training School at Burnhill Green. (Historic Military Press)

TRAINING NOTES.
29.m.m. SPIGOT MORTAR

HOME GUARD.
South Staffordshire Garrison.
Weapon Training School,
Burnhill Green.

BELOW: Another view of a Blacker Bombard. (Historic Military Press)

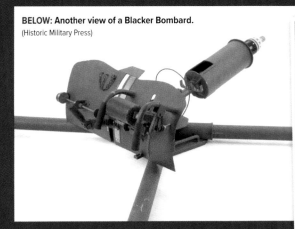

LEFT: Home Guards operate a Blacker Bombard during training at No.3 GHQ Home Guard School at Onibury near Craven Arms in Shropshire, May 20, 1943. (via Historic Military Press)

The Day the Bells Tolled

Most Home Guards had volunteered in the full knowledge that one day they might have to confront an enemy attack. When church bells were rung throughout the country on September 7, 1940, many believed that the moment had arrived.

Watching and waiting! A re-enactment of a private from the 21st Sussex (Eastbourne) Battalion on duty at the clifftop near Hope Gap, to the west of the town, watching for the impending invasion.
(Historic Military Press)

By the beginning of September 1940, the Luftwaffe had been pummelling the beleaguered fighter airfields in the south of England for over two months; the RAF appeared to be facing defeat. The Royal Navy, for its part, was virtually at a state of maximum readiness, and the army, whilst doing what it could to help construct the desperately needed anti-invasion defences, was training hard.

Then, without warning, on the afternoon of Saturday, September 7, 1940, the Luftwaffe deviated from its routine and launched its bombardment of London – the Blitz. This surprise move at first confused the defenders and then worried them: was this the precursor to an invasion?

There were other warning signs. The previous evening, for example, there had been a sighting of a fleet of sixty German warships, coastal craft and barges at sea off Calais – some of these vessels could be seen from the ramparts of Dover Castle. Whilst the infantry transports had been targeted by Bomber Command for a number of weeks, in what is now known as the Battle of the Barges, the presence of such large numbers at sea together was a worrying precedent. The Admiralty responded by ordering all cruisers, destroyers and small craft to be kept at immediate notice. Although the RAF also reacted by issuing its 'Alert No.1' warning – indicating "invasion imminent and probable within twelve hours" – in reality it had been operating close to, or at, its limit for so long that it made little difference to its operational status.

If further proof of an impending invasion was needed, it was found. Reconnaissance aircraft reported that German bombers and dive-bombers were massing in previously unseen numbers at airfields in northern France and Belgium, particularly between Calais and Ghent. "It may," suggested one assessment, "indicate their re-employment on a large scale in preparation for an invasion of the South and South-East coasts".[1] Likewise, on September 7, the Joint Intelligence Committee was advised that the number of barges being held in readiness at Ostend had risen from the paltry eighteen spotted on August 18 to a far more worrisome total of 270.

At the same time, an intercepted German Enigma signal, also dated September 7, contained plans for the laying of a huge smoke screen in the English Channel. Even the weather seemed to be on Hitler's side – one meteorological report stated that, during the weekend of September 6 and 7, "the Channel tides would be as favourable as at any time this year for a crossing".

The Führer himself encouraged such speculation through a speech he delivered in Berlin on September 4 to a hysterically cheering, all-female crowd of nurses and social workers: "When people are very curious in Great Britain and ask, 'Yes, but why doesn't he come?', we reply: 'Calm yourselves! Calm yourselves! He is coming! He is coming!'"[2]

A leaflet published to advise the public what action to take in the event of a German invasion. Carrying a message from the Prime Minister, this leaflet, issued by the Ministry of Information in co-operation with the War Ministry, is dated June 1940. (James Luto Collection)

ABOVE: **Prepared to face the enemy is this pair of improvised Home Guard armoured cars, both of which were operated by the men of the 7th Gloucestershire (Stroud) Battalion. This unit was fortunate in having a number of wealthy beneficiaries, with two local residents donating the vehicles that were used as the basis for the armoured cars, named** *The Eagle* **and** *Daniel.* (Courtesy of The Tank Museum)

GERMAN AGENTS ARRESTED

To add to the mounting air of concern at the War Office, just twenty-four hours earlier, during the night of September 3, 1940, the Germans made what is believed to have been their first attempt to land spies in Kent. Four agents came ashore having been landed, by rowing-boat, from a trawler located offshore. Two stepped ashore on the beach near Hythe, the other pair near Dungeness. Those at Hythe were quickly discovered by sentries from the Somerset Light Infantry, whilst, shortly after, one of the remaining two agents was marched into a nearby police station by an ARP Warden. The fourth spy remained at large for a little longer, not being discovered until the next morning.

When all four men had been rounded up, they were transferred to M.I.5's newly-opened interrogation centre at Latchmere House, near Ham Common in West London. No doubt acutely aware that time was of the essence, the centre's commandant was given one simple instruction in relation to their interrogation: "Truth, in the shortest possible time."[3]

In the event, it would seem that little pressure was needed, and it was soon established that the men had been despatched by the Abwehr, the German intelligence organization from 1921 to 1944, to observe and report on British troop depositions in the south-east. One or two of the spies also put their hope "in salvation by the imminent arrival of German soldiers on British shores". Not for nothing were the four men subsequently dubbed 'The Invasion Spies'.

It was against this deeply concerning background, and at the same time as the large armada of German bombers was heading north towards London, that the Chiefs of Staff gathered at the War Office. In discussing the implications of the sudden onslaught on the capital, all present agreed that the threat of invasion had increased. They had three levels of invasion alert available to them. Level 3 would indicate that "an attack is probable within three days", whilst Level 2 reduced the timescale to two days. Based on the evidence arranged before them, this august group duly concluded that "the possibility of

invasion had become imminent", that is to say alert Level 1. The British defences, they felt, "should stand by at immediate notice".[4]

The only means by which this could be achieved was the issue of the code-word *Cromwell*. This code-word, which at the instigation of General Edmund Ironside, the then Commander-in-Chief Home Forces, had superseded one with similar implications, *Caesar*, on June 5, 1940, was intended to alert its recipients to the fact that "conditions were suitable for invasion". It had never been intended to indicate that a German invasion was actually underway.

ABOVE: **Pictured on July 25, 1940, this collection of old vehicles had been placed on open fields as an anti-invasion, anti-landing, measure during the summer of 1940.** (Historic Military Press)

ABOVE: **An armoured car belonging to the Blackburn (Lancashire) Home Guard. Described as an Austin Riley type, it was photographed soon after the** *Cromwell* **alert on September 30, 1940. The gun mounted in the back appears to be a Browning automatic rifle.** (Courtesy of The Tank Museum)

CROMWELL ALERT

So, at precisely 20.07 hours on the evening of September 7, 1940, as bombs continued to rain down death and destruction on London, the Deputy Chief of Staff at GHQ Home Forces, no doubt mustering all the calm he could, authorised the despatch of *Cromwell*. The message was flashed to Eastern and Southern Commands, the GHQ Reserve (IV and VII Corps) and HQ London District. It was repeated, for information only, to all other Commands. For nearly four hours, *Cromwell* cascaded its way down through the United Kingdom's military chain of command.

When *Cromwell* was received, the reaction it generated varied widely throughout the nation, from almost nothing to the utterly dramatic. Unfortunately, a few recipients were

BELOW: **A third vehicle that was donated to the 7th Gloucestershire (Stroud) Battalion was transformed into an ambulance. It is seen here with the two armoured cars in August 1940, just prior to the** *Cromwell* **invasion alert.** (Courtesy of The Tank Museum)

under the false impression that *Cromwell* indicated that the invasion was actually underway – and they responded accordingly.

Eric Higgs was a member of a Home Guard platoon in the village of Lanlivery, near Lostwithiel, at the head of the estuary of the River Fowey in Cornwall. He would later recall how he received the invasion alert, as well as his subsequent actions: "There were just a few telephones in the parish at that time on odd farms, and a messenger arrived from a neighbouring farm to ours with the news from the Company's second-in-command that the code word *Cromwell* had been given. My task was to take my bicycle and hop over the fields to the next farm and to rouse that man, and so it went on throughout the parish. I would say that within half- to three-quarters of an hour, we Home Guards had mustered at our roadblock and had got it assembled.

"The road-block, on the A390 between St Blazey and Lostwithiel, was made up of railway sleepers and stretched halfway across the road leaving one side open. It was a very warm, quiet night. Anyone who has been there in that situation can recall the feeling of the unknown, wondering what we are going to face… I don't suppose – had the invaders come – that as Home Guards we would have stood a chance but, knowing the country, we could have delayed them for a while.

"The night dragged on, but it's peculiar how rumours get around. An Army truck came down the road from the St Austell direction. The driver stopped, and we said to him, 'Do you know anything?' 'I've just come from Truro,' he replied, 'and I've heard

ABOVE: **A member of the Rustington LDV or Home Guard pictured at his observation post on the South Coast in the summer of 1940.** (Courtesy of Mrs Mary Taylor)

rumours there that enemy troops are trying to get ashore at Marazion.' Now, you see, this was nothing but rumour. Someone, somewhere, had jumped the gun, and that was the sort of thing we were up against. We just didn't know what to think."[5]

THE BELLS RANG OUT

Across the country, road-blocks such as those deployed by Higgs and his comrades were hastily put in place, coils of barbed wire unravelled, stocks of improvised weapons, such as Molotov Cocktails, made ready, telephone-operators refused to accept non-official calls, and, most unhelpfully, church-bells rang. The latter only served to spread the confusion and alarm. Since June 13, 1940, church bells had been officially silenced and were only to be used in the event of an actual invasion. As one parish tolled its bells, the sound was heard in the next and they too rang theirs. Rapidly the word spread: the Germans are coming.

"In the Woking area," noted a columnist for the *Daily Herald* on September 9, 1940, "at one period six different sets of bells could be heard and the clanging went on for over two hours… In Basingstoke the tolling of the bells kept many people up all night, and when daylight broke, they were still under the impression that Britain had been invaded." At St Ives in Cornwall, the vicar, observing the local fishing fleet returning from the west instead of its usual route from the east, assumed that an invasion fleet was offshore. He unilaterally ordered his church bells to be rung – yet again setting in motion a predictable chain of events.

George Ames, a teenage volunteer in the Home Guard, was one of the many who heard the church bells tolling in Basingstoke that night. Having recently been appointed as the 'runner', or messenger, for his platoon, it was his role to cycle around the various homes or places of work of his comrades, passing on any orders or instructions.

"When the church bells began to ring," he later recalled, "I accordingly set off on what proved to be quite an eventful journey. Any German parachutists who were about that night would certainly have had a hard time of it from the housewives of Basingstoke, let alone the Home Guard, because they were out in force with broomsticks, rolling-pins and all manner of domestic implements and improvised weapons, including axes used for chopping wood and lethal kitchen knives. I was knocked off my bicycle and threatened countless times by these enthusiastic ladies but was offered cups of tea and showered with apologies once my identity was established. Given that I was riding about at midnight holding a large rifle their suspicions were understandable."[6] »

Issued on behalf of the   Ministry of War Transport

IMMOBILISATION OF VEHICLES IN THE EVENT OF INVASION

EVERY OWNER of a motor vehicle should be ready, in the event of invasion, to immobilise his car, cycle or lorry the moment the order is given. Failure to act promptly would give the enemy the chance to provide himself with transport.

It is important that owners of vehicles should understand now what they have to do, and satisfy themselves that they can carry out the order at any time without delay.

With a view to helping them, the Ministry of Transport gives the following information and

advice on what they must do when informed by the Police or through the Civil Defence services that immobilisation of vehicles has been ordered in their area :

PETROL VEHICLES

Remove distributor head and leads and empty the tank or remove the carburettor.

DIESEL-ENGINED VEHICLES

Remove the injection pump and connection.

Hide the parts removed well away from the vehicle.

P.T.O

LEFT: **The front of a small leaflet entitled 'Immobilisation of Vehicles in the Event of Invasion', which was issued on behalf of the Ministry of War Transport.** (James Luto Collection)

BELOW: **Surviving anti-invasion defences on the shoreline between Bawdey and Shingle Street on the Suffolk coast. Many pillboxes such as that seen here were often manned by men of the Home Guard.** (John New/Shutterstock)

"When daylight broke, they were still under the impression that Britain had been invaded."

ABOVE: The German preparations for their invasion of the United Kingdom, Operation *Seelöwe* (*Sealion*), included producing intelligence publications such as this. Dated August 15, 1940 and produced by the German Armies' General Staff in Berlin, it is a collection of photographs, including many taken from the air, of beaches and harbours along the South Coast – the potential landing beaches. (Richard Hunt Collection)

ABOVE: Dated June 30, 1940, this is another of the intelligence publications produced by the Germans in anticipation of Operation *Sealion*. It is in fact a collection of street maps for towns and cities throughout the United Kingdom. (Richard Hunt Collection)

In those areas of the country where confusion was the order of the day, the Army put its pre-arranged plans into action. In Eastern Command several bridges were demolished by the Royal Engineers. In Lincolnshire, emergency minefields were laid. In one case, this had dire consequences. At 06.05 hours on the morning of September 8, the Officer Commanding HQ Company of the 2nd Battalion Hampshire Regiment, Major Henry Phillips, was killed, along with his driver, Private Arthur Scovell, when their vehicle hit a land mine laid in the road. Both were buried in the churchyard at Mablethorpe, a short distance from where they died.

Also in Lincolnshire, a company commander of the Grenadier Guards also recalled how he responded to the alert: "I went round the billets, doubled the sentries, released the men in arrest and ordered the drummer to sound the alarm in the streets of Louth. I told the men the Germans might already have landed but where I had no idea. Our buses purred quietly in the field outside, their civilian drivers talking quietly to the Guardsmen, drinking cups of tea. Then, for there being nothing else to do, we returned to the billets, wrote our last letters and waited."[7]

THE HOME GUARD IS CALLED OUT

Though it had not been amongst the intended recipients of *Cromwell*, the Home Guard soon became aware of what was, or appeared to be, occurring. In true Home Guard style, it rose to the occasion with gusto. This was, after all, the very moment that hundreds of thousands of men had volunteered for.

In Leicestershire and Rutland, for example, the Home Guard received *Cromwell* at 21.25 hours from Northern Command. Throughout both counties, the volunteers 'stood to'. It may well have been this night

that Monica Turner, then a schoolgirl living in Stonesby, remembered her father Cecil Branston being called out: "My brother and I were awakened by a thumping on our cottage door. It was dad's boss in the Home Guard. 'Cis, come on, they have landed.' Well, mum got we kids up, wellies on, the lot. Dad came downstairs in his uniform. I say 'uniform' in the mild sense because his issue only got as far as a cap, a battledress about three sizes too big, and farm leggings. Dad said: 'All I've got is my hay fork.' He never got as far as a rifle issue. I will remember to this day my dad and his mate going off, as they thought, to meet Jerry with a hay fork and a shepherd's crook to fight."[8]

Along with the ringing of church bells, the banging on doors is one of the most readily recalled features of that late summer's night. For many Home Guards, the frantic rap on the door or window, disturbing a quiet rest or slumber, was the first indication that 'something was afoot'. Whilst we can look

ABOVE: Maps, essentially reprinted copies of contemporary British Ordnance Survey maps, were included in the German briefing document for Operation *Sealion*. The example seen here is of the area of the Sussex coast from Shoreham-By-Sea to Brighton. (Richard Hunt Collection)

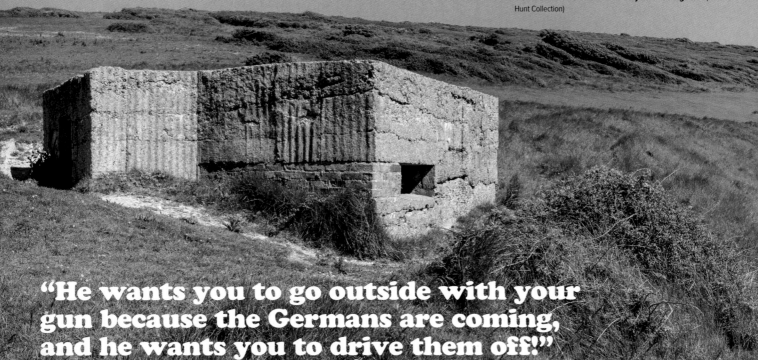

"He wants you to go outside with your gun because the Germans are coming, and he wants you to drive them off!"

ABOVE: The original caption to this image states: "Britain keeps her Army on the alert. A group of troops armed with rifles and automatic weapons take up a defensive position by a roadside." (Historic Military Press)

ABOVE: The remains of a roadblock that was constructed on the A281 in Shalford, Surrey, in the summer of 1940. This block was designed to take one end of a horizontal rail. (Historic Military Press)

back now with the benefit of hindsight and the full knowledge that the Germans never came, untold numbers of men, young and old, veteran and novice, left their homes believing that they were off to fight the enemy. A good many may well have thought, as they headed out, that they might not return and, never to see their loved ones again, they would die in the coming hours whilst serving King and Country.

Wilfred Hodgson, a teenager living in Camberley, Surrey, still vividly recalls that fateful evening: "It was a strange feeling lying in bed listening to the church bell and wondering what would happen to us all now that the invasion had really begun." With her father serving in the Home Guard and downstairs busily planning the town's defence, she noted that "the atmosphere in our house was very tense... the telephone rang incessantly".[9]

Serving in the 6th Wiltshire (Marlborough) Battalion, Don Dobson was a member of the section commanded by a Sergeant Pearce. He

ABOVE: A soldier stands guard by a pillbox in an unidentified location, August 1940. (Historic Military Press)

was fast asleep in bed when the drama began to unfold late in the evening of September 7. "I was woken by Dad," he later recalled, "who came into the bedroom shouting 'Can't you hear? Sgt Pearce is down there knocking the door down. He wants you to go outside with your gun because the Germans are coming, and he wants you to drive them off!' We had a sand-bagged emplacement at [a nearby] junction so we could control traffic coming along the Swindon road. It was about 2 o'clock in the morning and I went out to the position and waited there until eventually some of our chaps came by in a lorry, and I found out it had all been a false alarm."[10]

"THE SHORTEST DEFENCE IN HISTORY"

"At Llandudno," wrote Angus Calder, "the usual parades had been held, the usual guards posted, but long after the bar at the British Legion club where the Home Guard had their headquarters had been closed for the night, a Signals corporal was still teaching drill to a few enthusiasts. An officer answered a call from one of his Home Guard superiors, a colonel. 'The zone commander's been ringing,' the latter announced. 'I'm damned if I can make him out. All he'd say was *Cromwell*.'

"The corporal had stopped his demonstration and caught the word. With an exclamation, he ran off. Suddenly, the light dawned on the others. This meant invasion. Within a short time, the Llandudno Home Guard had been called out in their denim uniforms, and had been ordered to their battle stations — the town hall, the sea front, the golf links."[11] »

A surviving pillbox overlooking the beach at Cuckmere Haven on the South Coast. There is a variety of wartime anti-invasion defences still to be seen at this locality. (Chris Dorney/Shutterstock)

Training for the real thing. Home Guard volunteers are pictured staging an attack on an enemy 'tank' – in reality a corrugated iron mock-up – as they defend a concrete road barrier with Molotov Cocktails in August 1940. (Historic Military Press)

south east coast,' and he roared off to round up the other men.

"Other men might have reacted differently, but my reaction was to run into the house, tell them all that the invasion had started, and wrapping some bread in some paper thrust it into my pocket expecting to be away from home for a long time.

"All was chaos at the Lecture Hall. Home Guards were coming in from all over the area. They were roughly formed into groups and sent to all the strategic points in the village. I was sent to the railway bridge on Ellison Road. There used to be some waste ground there with a slight hollow in it. There we settled down to await events. We had been issued with 5 rounds of ammunition each, and I thought that if we didn't get some more ammunition soon it was going to be the shortest defence in history."[12]

"THERE WILL BE NO RETIREMENT"!

As the evening wore on, huge swathes of the country had been stood to arms – though the value of those arms was often debateable. At an army workshop in Stockton-on-Tees in County Durham, the best the officer in charge could do was arm his men with heavy spanners. At Cromer in Norfolk, trenches on the beaches were manned by young naval recruits who, whilst still in training, at least had rifles – even if they had barely seen one before. One Home Guard at Potters Bar, Hertfordshire, found himself reporting for duty with his wife's broom handle. Near Lewes in East Sussex, one farmer who found

Like their colleagues in the Llandudno Home Guard, the men of the 14th Company of the 25th London Home Guard also happened to be together on the evening of the 7th – the unit's first batch of the denim uniforms had been received and its issue was about to be made, as the company commander later noted: "Elaborate arrangements were made for the issue on September 7, every man was to sign for each

item received and the most precise records started. The Platoons did about a four-mile march, and were just enjoying a cup of tea when the siren went.

"As many warnings had been heard during the previous fortnight no notice was taken, and the issue was commenced. It was not long before it became obvious that this was the real thing, and parties were dashing out for parachuting Germans, crashed 'planes, etc., some with a denim blouse, flannel trousers, soft hats, and one civilian shoe and one Army boot." Such it was, this Home Guard later recalled, that his unit's "first great administrative test clashed with the first operational test". The aftermath, he added, was somewhat comical: "In the dawn of Sunday, September 8, the yard at the back of Company H.Q. was still strewn with civilian jackets and parts of denim uniforms."

Too young for the Regular Army, Joseph O'Keefe was amongst the earliest volunteers for the LDV in his home village of Dunston near Gateshead. He vividly remembered the events of that fateful Saturday afternoon in September 1940: "I had just stepped out of our house in Armstrong Street when a Home Guard despatch rider pulled up beside me. 'Your name is O'Keefe isn't it?'. 'Yes, why?' I said.

"'Report to the Lecture Hall at once. The invasion has started.' 'Surely you mean a practice exercise,' I said.

"'No', he shouted. 'They've landed on the

ABOVE: Coastal artillery guns such as that seen here 'somewhere in England' on August 26, 1940, were quickly manned following the issuing of the *Cromwell* code-word. (Historic Military Press)

ABOVE: Following the lessons learnt during the weekend of September 7-8, 1940, from the beginning of 1941 Invasion Committees were established in towns and villages nationwide. The intention was that these bodies would cooperate with the military and plan for the worst should, as their title suggests, an invasion take place and their communities be attacked, isolated or occupied. The members of committees typically included representatives of the local council, the Air Raid Precautions service, the fire service, the police, the Women's Voluntary Service and the Home Guard. The document seen here is a contact list for the Borough of Watford (Bradshaw Ward) Invasion Committee. (James Luto Collection)

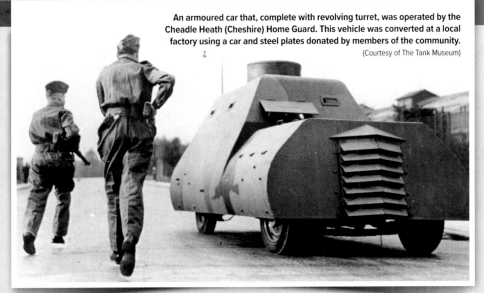

An armoured car that, complete with revolving turret, was operated by the Cheadle Heath (Cheshire) Home Guard. This vehicle was converted at a local factory using a car and steel plates donated by members of the community.
(Courtesy of The Tank Museum)

himself garrisoning a recently-completed pillbox, was in possession of rare riches – a rifle with a whole box of fifty rounds of ammunition. However, he was not greatly cheered by the arrival of an army officer who promptly declared: "There will be no retirement"![13]

Many a soldier and Home Guard lost a night's sleep as they peered up into the inky darkness watching and waiting for burly Nazi paratroopers descending from the night's sky. 'After that, all one could hear,' the *Daily Herald* reporter concluded, 'was the echoing and re-echoing of the Home Guard challenge "Who Goes There?", with occasional rifle shots when the challenged party failed to stop'.

Not every Home Guard, however, was convinced of the enemy's imminent arrival. One volunteer in the Norfolk Home Guard had, for example, refused to leave his bed. "I'll get up if he comes," he defiantly declared, "but I know he baint a-coming".

Those nearest to the enemy were perhaps most fearful of a German attack – and no one could get much closer than the coastal defence batteries around Dover Harbour. As soon as *Cromwell* was received, recalled Colonel B E Arnold, all the batteries were instructed to 'Stand To'. "All the guns of the defences were loaded," he wrote. "Additional trays of ammunition were brought up on the electric hoist on the Arm, and were stacked at the rear of the guns. We also primed all the hand grenades. These were issued to all ranks down to Bombardier, but I retained a half dozen for myself... Lookouts were doubled.

"Next morning was a clear bright day and, in fact, we could look right across the Channel to the French cliffs. Instead of a vast armada of ships approaching our shore, there

was not a vessel in sight and certainly no invasion fleet coming to surprise us."[14]

Indeed, as dawn gradually broke, the early light revealed to one and all that no German boots had set foot on British soil. It had all been a false alarm.

As the morning progressed, area by area, units were stood down – though *Cromwell* would not be completely cancelled for some time, after all the threat of invasion still remained. Slowly but surely the country returned to some semblance of normality.

For their part, the majority of those under arms in Britain had proven, despite the subsequent anticlimax, that they had been willing, if not fully prepared, to face a German invasion. The night's events also revealed many of the deficiencies which still remained in the nation's defences – shortcomings that could hopefully be rectified before the Germans did come.

If nothing else, as Winston Churchill later wrote, "it served as a useful... rehearsal for all concerned". This, of course, included the untold thousands of men in the ranks of the Home Guard.

NOTES

1. Norman Longmate, *Island Fortress: The Defence of Great Britain 1603-1945* (Grafton, London, 1993), p.511.
2. ibid.
3. T Crowdy, *Deceiving Hitler* (Osprey, Botley, 2008), p.40.
4. Winston Churchill, *Their Finest Hour: The Second World War Volume Two* (Reprint Society, London, 1951), p.257.
5. David Carroll, *Dad's Army: The Home Guard 1940-1944* (Sutton, Stroud, 2002), p.38.
6. ibid, p.39.
7. M Glover, *Invasion Scare 1940* (Leo Cooper, London, 1990), p.165.
8. Austin J. Ruddy, *To The Last Round: The Leicestershire and Rutland Home Guard 1940-1945* (Breedon Books, Derby, 2007), p.32.
9. Frank and Joan Shaw, *We Remember the Home Guard* (Hinckley, 1990), p.23.
10. Roger Day, *Look, Duck & Vanish* (Roger Day, Hungerford, 2011), p.36.
11. Angus Calder, *The People's War: Britain 1939-1945* (Panther, London, 1971), p.180.
12. Frank and Joan Shaw, ibid, p.165-6.
13. Norman Longmate, ibid, p.513.
14. Colonel B E Arnold, *Conflict Across the Strait* (Crabwell Publications, Dover, 1982), p.117.

British defenders, including those manning a 2-pounder gun, on duty on a South or East Coast beach, on the alert for any sign of an invasion, in the summer of 1940.
(Coloured by Jon Wilkinson)

MAIN PICTURE: A complete example of the Smith Gun and its limber. (Historic Military Press)

"[It was] a brute of a weapon, very heavy and awkward to handle."

Captain H G Smith of the 7th Essex Battalion Home Guard

Another view of a Smith Gun. (Historic Military Press)

WEAPONS OF THE HOME GUARD:
Smith Gun

The 'Ordnance Smooth-Bore, 3in. Mk.I', more commonly referred to as the Smith Gun, is probably one of the most unusual artillery pieces ever produced. Certainly, of the three so-called 'sub-artillery' weapons issued to the Home Guard – the others being the Blacker Bombard and the Northover Projector we have already covered – it is by far the least well-known.

The brainchild of Major (Retd.) William H Smith, the Managing Director of Trianco Ltd, the Smith Gun was, also borne out of Britain's dark days after the Dunkirk evacuation. Smith conceived the gun as a cheap and easily produced anti-tank weapon. By the end of 1940, the first prototypes had been completed by Trianco's engineers at their head office at Imber Court, East Molesey, in Surrey.

The Smith Gun underwent its first official trial on December 9, 1940. Conducted by the Superintendent of Experiments at Shoeburyness Ranges, the tests were described as being "of great interest". Despite further trials during early 1941, however, the Ordnance Board remained unconvinced about the viability or usefulness of the design. As with other Home Guard weapons, it was Winston Churchill, who, having been present at a demonstration, ordered that the gun be put into production, orders being placed by the end of the year.

On January 2, 1942, a letter from V Corps, to the Headquarters Home Guard Southern Command, advised that "an allotment of 180 Smith Guns will shortly be made to the Home Guard units of this Corps". Soon after, on April 20, 1942, Southern Command also noted that "some 3,000-5,000 Smith Guns can be made available for issue to Home Forces in the course of this year".

The Smith Gun was a simple smooth-bore, breech-loading, gun that ran on two 48-inch diameter metal disc wheels, both with solid rubber tyres. When going into action, the gun had to be turned over onto its right-hand concave wheel. The left-hand convex wheel therefore provided the gun crew with some degree of overhead protection.

The Smith Gun was intended to be operated by a gun detachment consisting of a commander and three gunners. Official advice was that the gun could be used in five main roles: close support of infantry; as a mobile reserve of fire power in defence; as a mobile or static anti-tank gun; in support of a mobile patrol; or, lastly, in defence of open spaces such as airfields.

Opinion of the Smith Gun was often far from favourable. Not least of its issues was the fact that the design had a particularly short effective range, or that it had a very low muzzle velocity and was considered by many to be inaccurate. Of much bigger concern was, as described in one technical manual, its "reputation for lack of safety". More precisely, as one battalion commander in Cornwall recalled, the Smith Gun had "a terrifying reputation for killing its crew". The main problem was faulty fuzes on the shells used – particularly in the early batches. Whilst a set of notes entitled the *Tactical Employment of the Smith Gun*, which was dated December 2, 1942, described it as a "simple, powerful and accurate weapon which, if properly handled, will add greatly to the fire power of the Home Guard", the historian of the 10th Wiltshire (Pewsey) Battalion was, on the other hand, much more dismissive, describing the Smith Gun as a "cross between a gun and an umbrella".

Despite the fact that it was not declared obsolete until December 1945, when it was withdrawn from service, the Smith Gun never attained the same status in the annals of the Home Guard afforded to its contemporaries.

ABOVE: A Smith Gun being displayed ready for firing. About 4,000 examples would eventually be manufactured, and of this figure, by the start of 1943, 3,049 were with the Home Guard. (via Historic Military Press)

RIGHT: A relic practice round found on a long-abandoned Home Guard range in Surrey. (Mark Khan Collection)

SMITH GUN IN ACTION THROUGH MOUSEHOLE

ABOVE: A picture taken from wartime training instructions showing how a Smith Gun might be deployed in an urban environment. (Historic Military Press)

LEFT: General Sir H E Franklyn, Commander in Chief Home Forces, looks on with Lieutenant Colonel H J Bretton, Battalion Commander of the 16th Kent (Gravesend) Battalion Home Guard, as one of the latter's Smith Gun teams goes through its paces. (With the kind permission of the Kent Messenger)

Mum's Army

It was unthinkable. How could women, the fairer, gentle sex, be trained to fight and kill? Yet it happened, and thousands of Women's Home Guard Auxiliaries did indeed take up arms in defence of the realm.

When Anthony Eden's appeal went out for local defence volunteers in May 1940, it was not only men that turned up at the police stations. Some, rather bewildered, desk sergeants were also confronted by women. One such was Edna Selwyn, a company secretary from Birmingham. She later remembered: "I went straight round there as soon as Anthony Eden finished. [The police sergeant] was quite horrified and said 'I had no idea there'd be any women'."[1]

The sergeant gave Selwyn the job of helping him to enrol volunteers, and,

in this way, she became one of the first 'unofficial' women to support the new force. However, it had not been the government's intention that women should join the LDV, but numerous local commanders certainly accepted women volunteers. Typically, these 'unofficial' women acted in auxiliary capacities, as secretaries, drivers, and in catering roles.

One unit which formally recruited women from the outset was the Upper Thames Patrol (UTP). An organisation that was created soon after the outbreak of war to patrol the River Thames from

Teddington to Lechlade, following the formation of the LDV the UTP was reorganised into two companies, one water-borne and the other for shore duties, in June 1940. Having become part of the Home Guard, at its height the UTP had 6,000 members, mainly Thames water-men but also civilians. Unable to recruit enough male personnel, the commanding officer recruited women who helmed boats and crewed alongside their male colleagues. In fact, on August 29, 1940, over 40 women joined the UTP in Wallingford, although this was never officially sanctioned.[2]

BELOW: A group photograph of personnel from 'K' Sector, London District, Home Guard HQ Signal Section, that was taken in November 1944. Note the high number of female volunteers – the so-called 'Mum's Army'. (Courtesy of the James Luto Collection)

Many fought against the unofficial arrangements that the women were placed in. Chief among them was Edith, later Baroness, Summerskill, the Labour MP for Fulham West and a leading parliamentary advocate of women in the Home Guard. In particular, she sought a more active role for women in the force. "Women should be enlisted into the Home Guard as fully combatant members of it," she demanded, "to man barricades, to go on reconnaissances etc. after being trained in the use of the rifle and, if necessary, in automatic weapons." The Secretary of State for War completely rejected her demands.

Also speaking out in parliament was the independent MP Eleanor Rathbone. On July 2, 1940, she used a debate on the LDV to raise the question of female recruitment – Summerskill also participated in this session. Rathbone asked the Secretary of State for War "whether he has considered the desirability of forming a women's force auxiliary to the Local Defence Volunteers, on lines similar to the women's services auxiliary to the Army, Navy and Air Force?". To this Eden replied: "I am aware of the patriotic desire of many women to serve in this way, and I am considering means of

RIGHT: Two female members of the Upper Thames Patrol, Mrs W C Thiele (right) and Mrs P Bartlett, pictured on duty in January 1941. Both had served as helmswomen in the Upper Thames Patrol since its inception. (Alamy)

giving expression to it."[3] Eden refused to be drawn further and steered the debate away from the subject.

Despite such a stance, there were increasing accounts of women being trained with weapons. This included a report in the summer of 1941 about a Home Guard factory unit in Tolworth, Surrey, where 'girls' working at the factory had for three months been drilling, marching and learning to use rifles with the men. In response to such developments, the War Office issued an order, news of which was published in *The Times* on November 12, 1941: "The War Office has sent an order to all Home Guard units that the training of women as unofficial Home Guard units has not been authorized. Weapons and ammunition in the charge of the Army or of Home Guard units must not be used for the instruction of women and the use of the name Home Guard is not permitted."

MORALE BOOSTER

Local units continued to recruit women in other capacities, for example, as drivers. By late 1942, as many as 50,000 women were serving, entirely unofficially, with the Home Guard. Then, on April 20, 1943 it was finally announced that women could be officially enrolled in the Home Guard. These women were to be between the ages of 18 and 65 and preferably older than 45

i.e. beyond usual child-bearing age, and could fulfil a number of specific duties which included driving, telephone operator, cook, and clerical and admin roles. They would be issued only with a small, plastic brooch badge, and would not be permitted to carry weapons, let alone train with them, despite the fact that from the start of the war women had trained with weapons.

The largest such organisation was the privately organised Women's Home Defence corps. The women of the WHD, which claimed 30,000 members in April 1943, undertook rifle training, and often practised on shooting ranges with local Home Guard units. One of those women was Ellen Baxter, who recalled her experiences at rifle practice. Ellen could only 'wink' with one eye, her right one: "When we used to have to do our rifle duties… I had to wear an eye-shield on my left eye as I couldn't wink. This caused a great deal of amusement. They said I would have to tell the Germans to wait while I put my eye-shield on."[4]

The women volunteers were initially given the rather unflattering title of 'nominated women', but this was later changed to Women's Home Guard Auxiliaries, the government setting a ceiling of 80,000 for the force. The only uniform that they were supplied with was a Bakelite brooch about two inches in diameter with the initials H G on it. »

"Most people take the view that they would like to kill at least one German."

ABOVE: Home Guards advance warily during an exercise near Exeter, August 10, 1941. Such offensive roles were generally denied to female members of the Women's Home Guard Auxiliaries. (via Historic Military Press)

BELOW: A plastic wartime 'economy' lapel badge issued to the members of the Women's Home Guard Auxiliaries. These were issued in 1943 and 1944. This example was manufactured by A. Stanley & Sons, Walsall. (Historic Military Press)

One of the many volunteers was Mrs Lois Baker who was a young clerk in the Air Ministry. Most of the men she worked with became officers and other ranks of the Air Ministry Battalion of the Home Guard. Lois and her co-workers had volunteered for fire watching and first aid duties but were keen to be more actively involved and join the Home Guard and seized the opportunity that the new rules represented. As part of the Air Ministry Auxiliary Section, the women paraded weekly, with some being detailed as cooks and others as signallers. They were also permitted a uniform of sorts in the form of navy blue boiler suits, navy caps, service helmet and respirator (locally-manufactured armbands were soon added). Baker and her colleagues were undoubtedly enthusiastic: "The highlight of one was a day out with the men on manoeuvres at Hatfield airfield bumping there in an army truck. We were given instruction and allowed to fire service rifles – vicious beats with a tremendous kick; in fact at the

first attempt I thought I might have died of shock!… I wonder how much support we could have given in an emergency, a real one? Fortunately, this was never put to the test but for us it was a wonderful morale booster."[5]

'KILL AT LEAST ONE GERMAN'

There continued to be widespread resistance to the idea of women using weapons, and officially they were not permitted to train in combat roles. It was pointed by those opposing this that in wartime, all civilians, women and men, suffered the threat of invasion and that it was illogical to deny women the right to join the Home Guard or for them to learn how to defend themselves.

This point was made by *Squadron Leader Eric Errington*, Conservative MP for Bootle, in a debate in the House of Commons: "In Russia women are right in the war. Why should not our women be taught the use of hand-grenades and revolvers with which they could protect themselves? Most people

take the view that they would like to kill at least one German."[6] In opposition to this, David Robertson, the MP for Streatham, declared that "a woman's duty is to give life and not to take it".

Nevertheless, in some instances, men encouraged women to join them in the Home Guard. One of these was Jacqueline Turney, whose father, a town mayor, formed a Home Guard company and enrolled her at the age of sixteen in 1943. She was one of seventeen, mainly young, women who trained as a signaller, learning Morse code.

Generally, the title given to the women's Home Guard, that of Auxiliaries, defined their roles. They were seen as merely being there to support the male military 'in the back room' and 'behind the lines'. When the Home Guard was disbanded in November 1944, there were still 32,000 Women Home Guard Auxiliaries.

NOTES

1. BBC People's War website, Article A4036240.
2. See www.thamesatwar.co.uk.
3. *Hansard*, House of Commons Debate, vol 362 cc644-7.
4. Penny Summerfield & Corinna Peniston-Bird, 'Women in the Firing Line', *History Review*, 9:2, pp.231-255.
5. Frank & Joan Shaw, *We Remember the Home Guard* (Ebury Press, London, 2012), pp.55-6.
6. *Hansard*, vol. 376, col. 108–9, Debate on the Address, 13 November 1941.

Blitz Gallantry

As the Germans intensified their assault on Britain's towns and cities after September 7, 1940, it was the Home Guard units in the urban areas, as opposed to the coastal regions, that suddenly found themselves quite literally on the front line.

The start of the Blitz brought new terrors to the streets of Britain's towns and cities. Following its beginning on September 7, 1940, the initial onslaught of Hitler's new bombing offensive was generally concentrated against London and the surrounding area. During October, London was not free of bombing for a single night. Then, in the latter half of that month, many of the nation's other big cities were attacked. Coventry and Birmingham were bombed heavily during the last fortnight of October, while Liverpool, Manchester, Hull and Glasgow also had their share.

The Blitz gave the men of the Home Guard an added purpose – particularly those in the urban battalions. Working alongside the police and ARP services, the Home Guards helped in rescue work, rendered first aid, roped off and secured the approaches to unexploded bombs,

mounted guard on damaged and dangerous properties, diverted traffic and evacuated civilians from unsafe areas – to list just a few of the many varied tasks to which they turned their hand. The 15th County of London (Bermondsey) Battalion, for example, maintained a contingent of 50 men at each sub-divisional police station every night throughout the Blitz. There were no known instances of a member of that battalion failing to turn up for duty during this stressful and dangerous period.

At the start of the Blitz, not every unit found itself suitably equipped to face the German bombs. The post-war history produced by No.6 Company, 23rd Middlesex (Edgware) Battalion notes how "one volunteer who lacked a steel helmet, to satisfy a nervous wife left home in the Blitz to come on duty wearing a piece of enamel-wear on his head, secured with a scarf". This Home Guard's colleagues over

in Bermondsey, in the east of London and where no less than three battalions had been formed (the 15th, 16th and 17th County of London), found themselves in a similar situation, as the historian Charles Graves noted: "To be privileged to see a party of H.G. calmly marching in fours (they had not yet learnt columns of threes) from Jamaica Road to Rotherhithe Tunnel with shrapnel and debris hailing down was a sight to be remembered for all time."[1]

Writing in 1943, Graves went on to provide a description of what the men faced as the Blitz unfolded: "There were days and nights when it seemed that everywhere must burn or collapse in ruin. Fires blazed everywhere. But nothing daunted these fellows. Out they intended to be, and out they were, doing all that could be done, shirking nothing. Many returned shocked, smoke-blackened, scorched, but they were out again after a cup of tea and a brief rest."[2] »

An inquisitive crowd is kept back from a bomb crater and damage in Threadneedle Street, in the City. Pictured on the morning of September 8, 1940, the damage was the result of the bombing the previous day and night – this being the official start of the Blitz. (Historic Military Press)

ABOVE: A member of the Home Guard on patrol through a quiet urban street. Note the blackout markings on the lamp post and walls. (Historic Military Press)

UNEXPLODED BOMBS

Each Home Guard endured different experiences of the Blitz. "By far the worst duty", recalled Alan Yeatman, a member of 'G' Section, No.11 Platoon, 11th Gloucester (City of Bristol) Battalion, "was guarding unexploded bombs. There were a lot of these during 1940/41, some 'duds', some time-fused, and there was no way of knowing which was which… All the houses around a UXB had to be evacuated immediately, many had windows blown in…

"The evacuation meant that you were entirely on your own – you and the bomb – no Wardens stopping by for a chat, or friendly householders bringing you out a cup of tea. Only the sound of running water from fractured pipes, and the green pinpoints of rats' eyes when the searchlights swung overhead. The police did the job till midnight, then we took over in two 3-hour shifts. A long time on a cold night, often during an air raid – I watched Bristol burn

on Good Friday 1941 while on this duty – and with distinctly unpleasant company."

Yeatman also noted how, for the Home Guards, the Blitz added greatly to the already heavy burden on their private lives: "Unlike the soldiers who had their regular off-duty periods, we, and the ARP services, had our day-time jobs to do as well. From 9 to 5, I was a clerk in the Bristol Corporation Electricity Dept; from 6 to 6, I was a part-time soldier. Once, a lady on a crowded bus gave up her seat to me! 7 in the morning, coming home after a rough night in the city, my uniform covered with rubble-dust, I was dozing off whilst strap-hanging… I still looked like a gangly schoolboy, with round glasses. Poor young lad!"[3]

RAINING STEEL

It was not only falling bombs that posed a danger for the Home Guard on duty in the Blitz. Almost certainly much of the 'shrapnel' that Charles Graves recalled

falling in Bermondsey was in fact fragments from exploding anti-aircraft shells. The dangers were very real, as one member of the 17th Hampshire (Portsmouth) Battalion reported to a Mass Observation team after the heavy raid on Portsmouth on the night of January 10/11, 1941: "You wouldn't dare going anywhere without your helmet on for fear of the shrapnel that was constantly falling." The same information gatherers also reported after this attack that among the city's residents the "fear was more of falling shrapnel than of the bombs".

Lieutenant L F Foster of the 15th Hertfordshire (St. Albans) Battalion graphically recalled why people came to be wary of the side-effects of the anti-aircraft barrage: "Sergeant Hitchcock was N.C.O. i/c [in charge] Guard at a road block when what was believed to be an unexploded bomb dropped on a house. Hitchcock broke his way into the house with his rifle butt while the Police were clearing all the inhabitants from the neighbourhood – and found that one of our own A.A. shells had fallen into the main bedroom and had killed a man instantly and seriously wounded his wife. He applied tourniquets to the woman, superintended her

ABOVE: Home Guards, ARP personnel, and many others, study the wreckage of the Dornier Do 17Z from 1/KG76, which, coded F1+FH, was shot down and fell to earth by Victoria Station on September 15, 1940. (Historic Military Press)

"There were days and nights when it seemed that everywhere must burn or collapse in ruin."

BELOW: Tower Bridge and London's docks on fire during the attacks on the first day of the Blitz, September 7, 1940. (Library of Congress)

Battling the Blitz over London, September 1940. As the original caption, dated September 14, states, "exhausts of fighter planes made white streaks in the sky over London during German air raids. The streaks stand out here above and to the right of the famous St. Paul's Cathedral." (Historic Military Press)

removal to an ambulance, and returned to duty without mentioning the matter, beyond a brief statement in his guard report to the effect that an A.A. shell had caused damage and casualties during his tour of duty. The details of his action were reported to me by one of the C.D. [Civil Defence] Ambulance Service two days later."

Whatever the cause, such scenes were played out across the country throughout the Blitz. On the night of December 22/23, 1940, a total of 272 tons of high explosive were dropped by the Luftwaffe on Manchester. One of the bombs struck a number of houses in Daisy Bank Road in the city's Longsight district. One of those demolished was No.46 – the home of 59-year-old Sergeant William McKee, of 'E' Company, 48th Lancashire (Manchester) Battalion. McKee was off duty when the bombs started to rain down.

One of the battalion's officers later recalled the events that night, and, in particular, the efforts of 'F' Company's Sergeant H. Landing, predictably known to all as 'Happy Landing': "In December 1940, a bomb demolished some nearby houses, and it was found that the house of a comrade, Sgt. McKee, had gone, and the family were buried under great piles of debris. Sixty-eight of the Platoon responded to the call for help and the indomitable courage and endurance of Sgt. Landing defies description. He worked night and day from Sunday night to the following Friday midday when all the bodies were finally recovered, and one daughter rescued alive." William McKee, his wife, and two sons had all been killed.

ABOVE: The Blitz begins – an observer watches an air battle over London during the early days of the Luftwaffe's onslaught, September 1940. (Historic Military Press)

"COOL COURAGE AND SELF-SACRIFICE"

For his actions in Daisy Bank Road, Sergeant Landing was subsequently represented with a Certificate of Meritorious Service. Another event in which a Home Guard was recognised for his gallantry in the Blitz relates to Section Commander George Inwood of the 10th Birmingham (Public Utilities) Battalion, which later became the 30th Warwickshire (Birmingham) Battalion. One of the most important industrial centres in Britain, Birmingham played a vital part in the nation's war effort. Aircraft, tanks and army vehicles rolled off the production lines of the city's factories, whilst many smaller workshops were involved in making items such as ammunition cases and grenades. Unsurprisingly, all this meant that Birmingham, the largest city outside of London, was a prime target for the Luftwaffe's attention. »

ABOVE: Home Guards, soldiers and ARP personnel gather at the crash site of the Heinkel He 111H-3, werke 5680, which came down ar Burmarsh, Kent, on September 11, 1940. The aircraft had been shot down by anti-aircraft fire over London. (Historic Military Press)

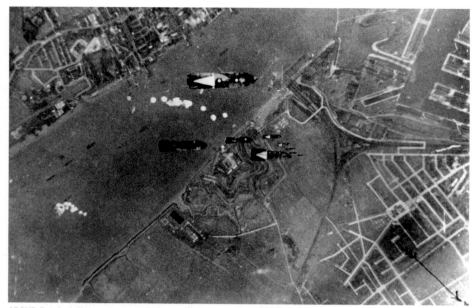

ABOVE: Bombs falling on the port of Tilbury, on October 4, 1940. The first group of bombs hit ships lying in the Thames, the second struck the docks themselves. (Historic Military Press)

One of these attacks occurred on the night of October 15/16, 1940. Whilst the raid was underway, 34-year-old Section Commander Inwood was asked by the police if he and his men would assist with rescue work in Bishop Street in the Five Ways area. A report in The Times of May 28, 1941, details what followed: "Taking charge of a party of six volunteers, he found that several people were imprisoned in a gas-filled cellar. A small hole was made, and Section Commander Inwood was lowered into the cavity. With great bravery he succeeded in bringing up two males alive. Although nearly exhausted, he entered the cavern a third time and was overcome by fumes. He was dragged out by one of his comrades, but despite the attention of a doctor and nurse, it was impossible to revive him. He showed the highest form of cool courage and self-sacrifice for others."

For his actions that night, Inwood was posthumously awarded the George Cross. His widow was presented with the medal

at an investiture at Buckingham Palace on October 10, 1941.

The second highest award of the United Kingdom's honours system, the George Cross was awarded "for acts of the greatest heroism or for most conspicuous courage in circumstance of extreme danger" not in the presence of the enemy. Instituted at the same time as the George Cross on September 24, 1940, the George Medal was intended for those acts where the services "were not so outstanding as to merit" the GC. One of the Home Guard recipients of the GM was Platoon Commander Reginald Cooke, of what was then known as F7 (Austin Aero Engine Co. Ltd.) Company, Birmingham Zone Home Guard. A member of an auxiliary bomb disposal squad operating at the Leebank Works of Messrs Burman Ltd., which was located in Highland Road,

Birmingham, Cooke was one of the first members of the Home Guard to be decorated specifically for bomb disposal work:

"On 26 October 1940, a 250kg bomb fell on the machine shop of Messrs Burman and failed to explode. The factory at that time was engaged on vital aircraft production work and so the bomb was given a high priority for clearance and a Royal Engineer detachment from 9 Bomb Disposal Company, R.E., under the command of Second Lieutenant R.H. Lee, was detailed to clear it.

"Despite the combined efforts of the Army and the auxiliary squad the bomb was not exposed until 28 October 1940, some 45 hours after it had fallen. Upon inspection it was found to have a clockwork long-delay fuse which was still ticking. In view of the time which had elapsed since the bomb had fallen, its detonation was probable at any moment.

"Second Lieutenant Lee cleared his men and the members of the auxiliary squad from the area and attempted unsuccessfully

ABOVE: Rescue workers, including ARP and Home Guard personnel, at work in Johnson Road, Bromley, after a Heinkel He 111, shot down by anti-aircraft fire, slammed into a number of houses in the street on November 9, 1940. Note how one of the men is carrying a bomb on his shoulder. (Historic Military Press)

to remove the fuse. After fifteen minutes' determined work he had to admit defeat and withdrew to consider the next move. In view of the importance of the factory it was decided to attack the fuse a second time but with less finesse and more brute force. (The fuse would be prized out with a crow-bar!) This could not be done by one person alone and Mr Cooke volunteered to assist. At this attempt they managed to break off the top of the fuse but the dangerous clockwork mechanism was still ticking and the bomb's detonation was imminent. It was then decided to flood the hole in which the bomb was lying in an endeavour to stop the clock. Second Lieutenant Lee and Mr Cooke completed this task together and to their relief the clock stopped, and the bomb was safely removed."[5]

Some Home Guards found themselves ideally suited to certain tasks in the Blitz, as the citation for the King's Commendation for Brave Conduct awarded to Volunteer F.

Stretcher bearers and medical personnel of the 24th Middlesex (Mill Hill) Battalion at work rendering first aid. (Historic Military Press)

ABOVE: A Home Guard exercise underway in London, August 1941. The original caption states: "Home Guards attack the Admiralty in exercises. A Home Guard detachment has successfully defended the Admiralty from an attack from two War Office companies of the same organisation, even though it was all just an exercise in military tactics. In this photo two of the defenders hurl hand grenades as members of the attacking party approaches." (Historic Military Press)

ABOVE: A Home Guard in action during the exercise around the Admiralty in August 1941. (Historic Military Press)

when the platoon left Claremont [near Esher] with 'T' Section, led by Sgt D. in the van. Sgt D. took his men down the lawn on the west side of the house and was turning round to pass a message back to his second-in-command when suddenly his words were lost as without warning he stepped off the edge of the lawn into a small moat... a fall of some three to four feet... Picking himself up, he proceeded. He had not gone another thirty yards when he disappeared again – this time walking over the edge of the anti-tank ditch, a drop of nearly ten feet."

At this point, it was decided that another Section should take over the lead. But this did not save the unfortunate Sergeant D., who lost contact with the leading Section and he and his men ploughed knee-deep in a 'stinking' bog. Sergeant D.'s next encounter was with a fence of pointed chestnut paling, tripping over which, he found himself face-down amid a colony of squealing pigs.

Despite all this, the exercise was completed successfully, and the platoon formed up and began to march off, with the resolute Sergeant D. recounting his night's mishaps to other section commanders. Suddenly, "in the middle of a sentence [he] once

more disappeared, this time over the edge of a steep cutting... Someone switched on a torch, and there was Sgt D. hanging for grim life to the protruding roots of a tree."[2]

MANNING THE GUNS
Following the launching of Operation *Barbarossa* in June 1941, when Hitler turned his attention eastwards, most began to believe that the likelihood of a full-scale German invasion was starting to diminish. America's entry into the war at the end of the year only exacerbated these views. The enemy had, it seemed, missed his opportunity.

Throughout the rest of the year, and into the next, the Home Guard continued to watch and learn. Training courses and schools sprung up throughout the country, and by the summer of 1942 it was noted that the General Service battalions, as most units were now referred, had reached such a state of efficiency that they had mastered the intricacies of battle drill with its sixty-five different words of command and thirty-four movements – all of which was disseminated down to the smallest squad. Few would disagree that this was a far cry from the early days of the LDV in 1940.

There were, though, many challenges to be faced. Chief among these was Parliament's passing, in December 1941, of the National Service (No.2) Bill. This widened the scope of conscription still further by making all unmarried women and all childless widows between the ages of 20 and 30 liable to call-up. Men were now required to do some form of National Service up to the age of 60, which included military service for those under 51. The main reason was that there were not enough men volunteering for police and civilian defence work, or women for the auxiliary units of the armed forces.

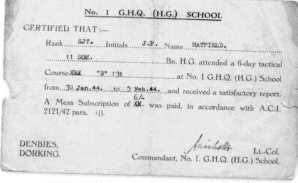

ABOVE: A certificate that confirms that Sergeant J F Hatfield attended a six-day tactical course at No.1 GHW (HG) School, which was located at Denbies near Dorking. Hatfield was serving in the 11th Somerset (Ilminster) Battalion. (Historic Military Press)

The bill contained provisions for compulsory enrolment in the Home Guard. The maximum number of hours to be completed each month by those in the organisation was set at 48. This was, noted the Home Guard historian Charles Graves, "regarded with some amusement by members of the Home Guard Battalions who were doing anything over sixty hours a month already".

MANNING THE GUNS
Towards the end of 1941 the demand on the Regular armed forces to continuously source more manpower, particularly for overseas service, led to the War Office deciding that men from the Home Guard should be trained for use on certain defensive duties. Among these steps, it was decided in the summer of 1942 to use members of the Home Guard to man some of the emergency coastal defence batteries that were situated within an individual battalion's area. In doing so, this would release valuable members of the Royal Artillery. Not all coastal batteries were handed over to the Home Guard – the major, established, peacetime forts were to remain under the control of the Regular Army. Others, such as those in less strategic positions, would be placed onto a 'care-and-maintenance' basis only. »

ABOVE: Corporal John Tough, a member of the 1st Northumberland (Berwick) Battalion, pictured at Lindisfarne armed with a P.14 rifle on June 30, 1942. (Historic Military Press)

ABOVE: A Home Guard unit pictured during a march past. A note accompanying the image states that this is likely to be a battalion of the Welsh Home Guard.

If we take West Sussex as an example, we know that the instructions to facilitate this transfer to Home Guard gun crews were issued in August 1942. Initially, the Royal Artillery garrisons were to be replaced at three emergency coastal batteries in the county. These were the gun sites at Worthing, which was to employ men from the 5th Sussex (Worthing) Battalion, Littlehampton, using the services of the 6th Sussex (Arundel) Battalion, and at Bognor Regis, to be manned by the 8th Sussex (Bognor and Selsey) Battalion. Each battery was to have a Home Guard establishment of two officers and 70 other ranks, whilst each individual shift was required to consist of a minimum of one officer and seven men.

Eventually, the men who had volunteered for such duties would receive special unit designations introduced for the coastal artillery batteries. By way of an illustration,

the emergency battery at Bexhill-on-Sea, East Sussex, was given the designation 301 Coast Battery, Home Guard. The Home Guard coastal artillery units remained on duty until they were stood down on September 11, 1944.

DEFENDING THE SKIES

At the same time as the Home Guard began manning coastal artillery guns, other members were being directed, or recruited (thanks to the 1941 legislation), to serve on anti-aircraft batteries. The training of Home Guards on the 3.7-inch anti-aircraft gun was undoubtedly an ambitious, and ultimately very successful, scheme. Aimed only at the General Service battalions, "preliminary training took place in drill halls during the winter or inclement weather, and consisted of loading, laying, firing, and plotting…

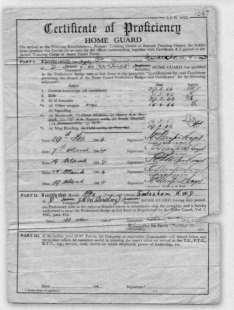

ABOVE: Evidence of the growing professionalism of the Home Guard. This is the Home Guard Certificate of Proficiency issued to Private K Goodenham, of 'D' Company, 5th Sussex (Worthing) Battalion. (Historic Military Press)

"Since June 1942… numbers of practice camps where live ammunition could be fired over the week-end were provided. It was estimated that if a Home Guard attended four training periods a week, apart from voluntary parades at the week-end, he would be operational on 3.7s within a few months. This training period was intense, and ex-gunner officers from the last war said in many cases that they learnt more real gunnery in two months than they did in two years in the Great War."[3]

The first victory by a Home Guard manned battery occurred on December 14, 1942, when 110 Battery, based on Tyneside, shot down a German bomber. The London-based anti-aircraft batteries did not fire at the enemy until January 17, 1943.

In 1942, the activities of the Home Guard anti-aircraft gunners had also been extended to include a new type of weapon – the 3-inch Rocket Projector, an anti-aircraft weapon which was commonly referred to as the 'Z' Battery. The No.2 Mk.1 Rocket Projector

ABOVE: General de Gaulle inspecting a Home Guard unit. The cloth insignia suggests that this is possibly the 11th North Staffordshire Battalion. (Historic Military Press)

THE REAL DAD'S ARMY

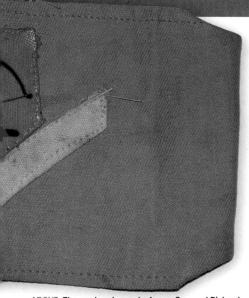

ABOVE: The armband worn by Lance Corporal Richard J Lilley whilst he served in 197/104 (City of London) 'Z' Battery, until transferring to the Lincolnshire Home Guard for work reasons. (Historic Military Press)

ABOVE: A heavy anti-aircraft unit of the Cheshire Home Guard in action. The Cheshire Home Guard had two heavy anti-aircraft batteries – the 71st Cheshire Home Guard Heavy A.A. Battery and the 72nd Cheshire Home Guard Heavy A.A. Battery. (Historic Military Press)

ABOVE: Members of a Home Guard-manned anti-aircraft rocket or 'Z' Battery load one of their launchers on Merseyside, July 6, 1942 (via Historic Military Press)

ABOVE: Members of the Home Guard in Waterlooville form a Guard of Honour for Admiral Sir William James, C-in-C Portsmouth, during Warship Week, March 8, 1942. (Historic Military Press)

ABOVE: An unusual duty for one Home Guard unit. Here, the first contingent of US Women's Army Auxiliary Corps officers and enlisted women to arrive in the UK is greeted on the quayside at Gourock by the pipe band of the 7th Battalion Scottish Home Guard, May 11, 1943. (NARA)

could fire one or two 3-inch rockets. Four guide rails were used, two to a rocket on each launcher. Two men laid each rocket, one traversing on the left, the other elevating on the right. Each battery retained regular gunners from the Royal Artillery to assist in training and maintaining standards. The age limit for Home Guardsmen to be posted to the 'Z' Batteries was 60, whereas it was 40 for those deployed to the conventional anti-aircraft guns and coastal defence batteries, because of the heavier ammunition.

The first rocket batteries manned by the Home Guard became operational in Kent and London. The 101st Kent Home Guard 'Z' Battery, for example, was formed on July 14, 1942, though initially it was known as 178 'Z' Battery, or, by its men, as the 'Gillingham Battery'.

Recruiting for all of the Home Guard anti-aircraft detachments was strong – at this stage of the war it was considered by many that this would be the only way by which, as a Home Guard, they would be able to 'have-a-go' at the enemy. From June 1942, in London alone enrolment of anti-aircraft gunners was running at several thousand men per month. From this number, men were drawn either for service on the standard 3.7-inch anti-aircraft guns or for the newer 'Z' Batteries.[4] Within a year of the decision being taken to utilize the Home Guard, a staggering 111,917 of its number were in anti-aircraft units, a figure that would rise further, to 141,676, by the late summer of 1944.[5]

All Home Guard gunners were expected to carry out a specified number of duties per month. The duty crews would be collected, or arrive, on site at about 20.00 hours, and remain on duty until 05.45 hours the following morning. They would sleep in huts on site, be fed and watered and only man the launchers during the course of training, or

upon sounding of the battery alarm. Service in the anti-aircraft units had revitalised the enthusiasm of many Home Guards to such an extent, that one of the difficulties battery commanders faced was preventing men who were not on duty from cluttering up the gun site when the alarm sounded.

THE END IN SIGHT

Before its disbandment, the Home Guard numbered in excess of 1.4 million men and women. It had become well-equipped, well-trained and highly disciplined along regular military lines. Indeed, each Home Guard battalion had become affiliated to its British Army county regiment. Though it never had to confront the invasion it was formed for, it served a newer purpose of releasing regular army units from home defence freeing them up for overseas operations.

The Home Guard also assisted with local community civil defence and generated a sense of commitment among society in general – even the young and the elderly could feel part of the war against Hitler. It also brought order and discipline to localities and gave many a sense of purpose; all members could feel they had 'done their bit'. Overall, the members of the Home Guard had demonstrated that they were just as willing as their full-time counterparts to sacrifice their lives in defence of King and country.

NOTES

1. *Hansard*, House of Commons Debate, November 6, 1940, vol 365 cc1347-54.
2. Norman Longmate, *The Real Dad's Army, The Story of the Home Guard* (Amberley, Stroud, 2012), p.134.
3. Charles Graves, *The Home Guard of Britain* (Fleet Street Press, London, 1943), p.165.
4. Richard Hunt, *Uniforms of the Home Guard* (Historic Military Press, Storrington, 2002), p.16.
5. Stephen M. Cullen, *In Search of the Real Dad's Army* (Pen & Sword, Barnsley, 2011), p.146.

The Ultimate Sacrifice

Many of those who served in the LDV and Home Guard would, like those in the regular armed forces, pay the ultimate price.

On June 6,1946, the Prime Minister, Clement Atlee, presented Parliament with a White Paper which contained "figures showing the strengths and casualties of the Armed Forces and auxiliary services of the United Kingdom during the war". Included within this document is a section relating to the Home Guard. According to the statistics, between its formation (as the LDV) and August 14, 1945, the organisation suffered a total of 1,763 casualties "attributable to service". Of these individuals, 1,206 had died of wounds, injury or illness, whilst a further 577 had been wounded.

However, as is often the case with the Home Guard, nothing is that simple or clear cut.

According to the Commonwealth War Graves Commission, it officially commemorates the death of 1,047 Home Guards who are listed as 'service casualties'. The CWGC's records also reveal that a further 1,087 Home Guards been killed whilst off-duty, almost entirely the victims of air raids, and that these individuals are, therefore, commemorated within the relevant civilian Roll of Honour.

THE FIRST TO FALL

The first casualty occurred with a few days of Eden's appeal for volunteers. A 33-year-old married man, Thomas Lyon was serving in the LDV as part of a factory unit defending the works in Dumbarton where he was employed

as a foreman – some accounts describe him as a ship-worker. On Sunday, June 2, 1940, Lyon was, noted a subsequent report in the *Daily Record*, "in a part of a building divided off by a partition. During instruction on rifle mechanism which was being given on the other side of the partition a rifle went off. The bullet passed through the partition and entered Lyon's neck. He was taken to Glasgow Western Infirmary where he died."

A survey of a random selection of 20% of the wartime fatalities reveals that in the first half of the war, until the summer of 1942 at least, the number of Home Guards accidentally shot accounted for 4% of those killed. By the second half of the war, this

This memorial on *Corbyn's Head i*n Torquay commemorates the death of four members of the 10th Devon (Torquay) Battalion who were killed in an explosion involving a 4.7-inch coastal artillery gun on August 11, 1944; a fifth Home Guard died of his wounds eight days later. (Courtesy of Sue Mitchell)

"It is... in the field of human relationship that the Home Guard will have left its most impressive mark."

ABOVE: Members of the Cheshire Home Guard pictured during the stand down parade in Chester in December 1944. The men of 'F' Company (Railway Unit), 6th Cheshire (Chester) Battalion are leading. (Historic Military Press)

Home Guard would be stood down with almost immediate effect. Arrangements would be made for us to hand in our uniforms and equipment at a later date. His statement was delivered coldly and clearly and was received by everyone present in total silence. I don't think that even the officers had any prior knowledge of this decision out of the blue.

"It is strange that nobody had given a thought to the probability of this event. After all, we were winning the war and the conflict would not go on forever. Neither would the need for our services, of course, yet we had not foreseen this sudden, almost brutal, announcement. In civilian terms, it was similar to a manager walking up to an employee and saying 'You're fired!'."[4]

At the time of its effective disbandment in September, the Home Guard, not counting the female Auxiliary Units, numbered 1,727,095 men (the peak figure of 1,793,000 had actually been reached in March 1943). Many others, during its four years of existence, had passed through its ranks, generally leaving because they had become of age to join the Regular forces or because they were too old. This huge army cost surprisingly little, the average annual cost per Home Guard in 1944 has been put at just £9 5s., whilst the total Home Guard budget for a year was only £16,600,000, roughly equal to a single day's expenditure on the war effort.[5]

MARKING THE DAY
The formal stand down came on December 3, 1944, with a parade in London through streets lined with cheering crowds, of 7,000 representatives from every single Home Guard battalion throughout the country, the salute being taken by King George who, with the Queen and their two princesses, stood for more than an hour as the as the troops marched past.

The crowds were, reportedly, no less than 10 feet deep everywhere and up to 20 to 30 in many parts, as the Home Guard marched from the assembly point in Hyde Park, through Hyde Park Corner Gate, Regent Street, Oxford Street and Marble Arch before returning to Hyde Park to be dismissed. »

ABOVE: Major H W Littleton-Geach leads a platoon from the 18th Devon (Saltash) Battalion during the Stand Down parade at Plymouth Hoe, December 3, 1944. (via the James Luto Collection)

THE PARISH CHURCH OF ST. MILDRED
TENTERDEN

2nd (Charing) Battalion Kent Home Guard

A SERVICE OF
RECOGNITION
OF
THE HOME GUARD
on the occasion of the "Stand-Down" Parade
ON 3rd DECEMBER, 1944.

"To toil and not to seek for rest
To labour and not to ask for any reward."

LEFT: Church services were also widely held at the time of the Home Guard's Stand Down. This order of service was printed for such an event attended by the 2nd Kent (Charing) Battalion. (Historic Military Press)

Souvenir

Stand Down of the
HOME GUARD
The Hoe   Plymouth
Sunday, 3rd December, 1944

RIGHT: The souvenir programme produced to accompany the parade marking the stand down of the Home Guard in Plymouth, December 3, 1944. (Historic Military Press)

ABOVE: The souvenir programme produced for a Farewell Smoking Concert arranged by the 101 Bucks Home Guard Rocket Anti-Aircraft Battery to mark their stand down. The event was held in Slough on December 1. (Historic Military Press)

According to one Home Guard officer, "It was as if London was saying with one voice: 'We know, we understand, we appreciate all the hard work you have put in, all the nights and weekends you have given up to make yourselves efficient soldiers in your spare time. We know what you might have been called upon to do for us, and we know you were ready and willing and anxious to give your lives if need be in protection of your country.'"[6]

A reporter for the *Daily Express*, Grace Herbert, wrote an account of the parade which described the sentiments felt that day: "A spectator can stand only at one place along a route, see one aspect of a marching man's face, one set of expressions – I felt a strange, unusual wish to cry. Why? These were ordinary men, our grocers, bank managers, husbands, sons. Men we see every day.

"But for this day they were uplifted into something different. They wore greatcoats and tin hats, some carried new rifles, others had last-war rifles. Some wore new boots which were hurting them; some were young – very young; some were old – though not too old. Men of 70 walked beside boys of 17. And they were comrades. It was the comradeship, not the militancy, of this procession which made me want to cry."

It was the subject of comradeship that an editorial in *The Listener* of December 7, 1944, also focused on: "It is… in the field of human relationship that the Home Guard will have left its most impressive mark. To citizens who have voluntarily formed themselves into military units and have drilled and exercised together, the distinctions of class will have less meaning than they ever had before. To the departmental chief who may perhaps have served as a private in the ranks, to the commissionaire or liftman who may very well have been his platoon sergeant, to the chauffeur who may have been an officer, to his employer who may never have risen

above the rank of corporal… to all these and to thousands like them, the experience in the Home Guard will have given not only a wider range of friends and acquaintances but also in most cases a broader and more generous outlook on their fellow creatures." The writer concluded by noting that, "When the country was in mortal danger the ranks closed; all stood together".

That evening there was also a 'Home Guard Stand Down Concert', given by the *Daily Mail* and which included stars such as Elsie and Doris Walters, Vera Lynn, Cicely Courtneidge, Violet Loraine, George Robey and Tommy Trinder. There was some poignancy in this list of names, as the last of those stars, Tommy Trinder, had sent his little motor yacht, *Chalmondesleigh*, to rescue the British troops from Dunkirk four years earlier. Home Guard units across the country also celebrated the occasion with 'Stand Down' suppers or their own parades.

ABOVE: Despite the Stand Down, the comradeship developed in many units over the four years of the Home Guard's existence continued – as this invite to a social event held in May 1945 testifies. It was presented by the Old Comrades' Association of No.4 Platoon, 'B' Company of the 25th Middlesex (Enfield) Battalion. (Historic Military Press)

"When the country was in mortal danger the ranks closed; all stood together."

BELOW: The men of 'A' Company, 9th Sussex (Shoreham-by-Sea) Battalion gather for a final group photograph on December 19, 1944. (Historic Military Press)

ABOVE: The menu card for the farewell dinner held by the men of 'D' Company, 5th Sussex (Worthing) Battalion which was signed by many of those present. (Historic Military Press)

ABOVE: Members of the 7th West Riding (Leeds) Battalion pictured during a function which is believed to be a farewell dinner. Note that the individual on the right is wearing Royal Flying Corps wings above his medal ribbons. (Historic Military Press)

ABOVE: Arranged by the 32nd Surrey (Croydon) Battalion Home Guard, this image illustrates just how far the organisation came in its four years. (via Historic Military Press)

THE KING'S SPEECH

Naturally, the King wanted to ensure that the Home Guard learnt of his gratitude. This came in two ways – a special written message issued on November 14, and a broadcast made on the BBC on the evening of December 3. In the latter the King said the following to all Home Guards: "Over four years ago, in May 1940, our country was in mortal danger. The most powerful army the world had ever seen had forced its way to within a few miles of our coast. From day to day we were threatened with invasion.

"In those days our Army had been gravely weakened. A call went out for men to enrol themselves in a new citizen army, the Local Defence Volunteers, ready to use whatever weapons could be found and to stand against the invader in every village and every town. Throughout Britain and Northern Ireland, the nation answered that summons, as free men will always answer when freedom is in danger. From fields and hills, from factories and mills, from shops and offices, men of every age and every calling came forward to train themselves for battle…

RIGHT: The menu produced for a meal held by the company commanders and their 2/ICs of the 6th (Fife) Battalion, on December 19, 1944, to mark the Stand Down. (Historic Military Press)

"For most of you – and, I must add, for your wives too – your service in the Home Guard has not been easy. I know what it has meant, especially for older men. Some of you have stood for many hours on the gun sites, in desolate fields or wind-swept beaches. Many of you, after a long and hard day's work, scarcely had time for food before you changed into uniforms for the evening parade. Some of you had to bicycle for long distances to the drill hall or the rifle range.

"It was well known to the enemy that if he came to any part of our land, he would meet determined opposition, at every point in his advance, from men who had good weapons and, better still, knew how to use them. In that way the existence of the Home Guard helped much to ward off the danger of invasion. Then, too, our own plans for campaigns in many parts of the world depended on having a great citizen force to help in the defence of the homeland. As anti-aircraft and coastal gunners, sentries at vulnerable points, units for dealing with unexploded bombs, and in many other ways, the Home Guard have played a full part in the defence of their country."

In his last Order of the Day, Colonel Crombie of the 5th Devon (Bideford) Battalion explained to his men just what the Stand Down meant: 'Though Stood Down we shall not be quite *Out* as we may be recalled in an emergency to our old stations; and I am sure that in such an event, we shall be very glad to get once more into our armour…'[7] Across the nation, the Home Guards were reminded to keep their weapons and uniforms ready for use.

The Home Guard was finally, completely, disbanded on December 31, 1945. Though it was not realised at the time, this, though, was far from the end of the story.

NOTES
1. S.P. Mackenzie, *The Home Guard* (Oxford University Press, Oxford, 1996), p.130.
2. David Carroll, *Dad's Army* (Sutton, Stroud, 2002), p.101.
3. Frank and Joan Shaw, *We Remember the Home Guard* (Ebury Press, London, 2012), p.341.
4. David Carroll, ibid, p.104.
5. Norman Longmate, *The Real Dad's Army* (Amberley, Stroud, 2012), p.152.
6. *History of the Cheshire Home Guard from L.D.V. Formation to Stand-Down, 1940-1944* (Gale & Polden, Aldershot, 1950), p.154.
7. Norman Longmate, ibid, p.158.

Cold War Home Guard

As the Cold War heated up and the prospect of war with the Soviet Union grew, fears of Fifth Columnists and enemy parachutists were raised once again. To some, the solution was to re-introduce the Home Guard.

MAIN PICTURE: **The men of the Billingshurst, West Sussex, Home Guard parading through their village high street, possibly to mark the organisation's Stand Down in December 1944. Within a few years some of these men might well have volunteered for the 'new' Home Guard.**
(Historic Military Press)

Almost as soon as the Second World War had concluded, a new enemy emerged in the shape of the Union of Soviet Socialist Republics. Communism and democracy were diametrically opposed political philosophies, and it was the aim of the former to establish world-wide control which, in its view, would best serve the needs of mankind. The threat from communism in the Cold War era, what some called the 'Red Scare', was as keenly felt as that from fascism had been just a few years earlier. The assessment was that if the Soviet Union invaded western Europe, the Red Army would quickly sweep up to the Channel ports as Hitler had done in 1940. This time it would be thousands of Soviet parachutists that might be dropped on the UK.

The Labour Government, which had replaced the war-time Conservative-led coalition in 1945, saw the more extreme left parties in Britain as potential Fifth Columnists and had toyed with the idea of bringing back the Home Guard. The first official step was a paper written by the Director of Military Operations in November 1948, before, in 1950, questions were asked about such a measure in the House of Commons. But it was the outbreak of the Korean War in 1951 which finally brought matters to a head. During the October general election campaign of that year, the Conservatives powerfully advocated the reintroduction of the Home Guard. Winston Churchill's Conservatives swept to victory and quickly set about re-establishing the Home Guard.

A Home Guard Cold War era lapel badge, circa 1953.
(Historic Military Press)

"The Home Guard appears to have struck the man in the street as both anachronistic and unnecessary."

On December 7, 1951, the Home Guard Act came into being. It was planned that its strength would be limited to 600,000 in peacetime, with a further 400,000 being recruited in times of war. All those who came forward were to be volunteers who would serve without pay, be subject to military law and be required to sign up for a period of two years. After this time, the volunteers would be eligible to "re-engage from time to time for a period of one year". Both men and women were eligible, and all had to undertake a minimum of 15 hours training every three months.

MORE CHIEFS THAN INDIANS
The Second World War had left Britain virtually bankrupt and rationing was still in force. Arming and equipping such a large

body of men and women would have placed a heavy financial burden upon the Treasury and the target strength was quickly scaled down to just 125,000. Of these, it was decided that 100,000 men would be required east of a line drawn from Flamborough Head to Selsey Bill, with the other 25,000 serving west of that line. Special tasks would be allocated in designated areas where the Government considered likely targets to be situated.

Recruiting for the new Home Guard, though, was very much slower than had been the case in 1940 and most units did not reach even the reduced size envisaged. One commentator explained why this was the case: "In the age of the hydrogen bomb and successive crises which never actually resulted in war, the Home Guard appears to have struck

the man in the street as both anachronistic and unnecessary." By February 18, 1952, only 28,120 of those men in the street had registered to join and by March only an average of 4,000 men a month were signing up.

Little changed over the following years and by early 1953 there was still only around 29,000 men still in service. These small numbers created an anomaly, in that officers and NCOs were required to lead sections and platoons, but each had precious few men to command. The term 'more Chiefs than Indians' applied to many units and of those 29,000 men under arms, 9,000 were officers. One Home Guard of that time, Roger Ray, a schoolmaster at Ashfold House preparatory school situated in Sussex between Horsham and Haywards Heath, recalled: "To carry » out [our] duties of helping to defend airfields, combating airborne and seaborne raids, protecting vulnerable points against sabotage and rendering help to Civil Defence, the ten men [of our unit] were kept on their toes. In charge of this army, half of them ex-wartime men, was Captain Richard Sykes, joint headmaster of the school. Promotion was fairly rapid, and I think there was only one private when we disbanded."[1]

The cost of maintaining the Home Guard in the years of austerity following the Second World War continued to be a pressing issue for the government, and in March 1955 the maximum level of the force was reduced to 55,000, even though this was still far beyond the numbers actually enrolled.

CHURCHILL'S 'OBSESSION'

There was, by 1955, increasing complaints that the Home Guard was a waste of taxpayers' money, especially as there was already in existence a Civil Defence Corps as well as the Territorial Army. Foremost among these was the Labour MP for Birmingham Aston, Woodrow Wyatt, who argued that the Home Guard would be of no value whatsoever in any modern war and only continued in being because it was Churchill's

ABOVE: Lieutenant General Lashner Whistler, General Officer Commanding-in-Chief of the Western Command, with local Home Guard commanders at Oswestry, March 31, 1954. (National Library of Wales)

ABOVE: A Home Guard recruitment poster from 1952. RIGHT: Another Cold War era Home Guard badge, that of the Isle of Man Home Guard with the Queen's Crown. (Both Historic Military Press)

"Became very popular and grew rapidly in personnel and in territory."

'obsession'. He also made the point that the members of the Home Guard worked during the day and that it could not be expected that, "an enemy would so conveniently arrange his aerial attacks… only during the night-time".

Wyatt claimed that the government was wasting £600,000 a year upon the Home Guard, pointing out that, "the adjutant-quartermaster in the Home Guard now receives £670 a year upon being first engaged, and an extra £35 every three years. I have here a letter from a man who served as adjutant-quartermaster in the Home Guard for two and a half years. He says: 'I realised what a racket it was.' Referring to the adjutant-quartermaster, he says: 'His work can easily be done in 2–3 hours per day and he only normally has one evening parade per week, of approximately two hours, apart from an occasional shoot on the local range on Sunday morning generally, and not often in the winter.' It is clear, that about 550 persons are being paid £670 a year [the average male weekly wage at that time was £217] or more for doing practically nothing. This really is a scandal."

In a debate in the House of Commons in March 1955, Wyatt concluded that: "The Home Guard has been a complete fiasco. There are very few people in the battalions, and it is very stupid to continue with an organisation which has no function in the future, has had no function since the end of the war."[2] There was little the government could do to challenge such comments and, in December 1955, the Home Guard was reduced to a reserve cadre and was finally disbanded for a second time on July 31, 1957.

THE HOME SERVICE FORCE

It might be thought that following the rather pitiful efforts at re-establishing the Home Guard in the 1950s, no further consideration would be given to creating such a body again. But, on March 3, 1982, with the Soviet Union's armed forces having become the largest in the world, the government announced the formation of a Home Service Force, which was to be linked to the Territorial Army. It was intended to consist largely of men with considerable regular service experience. The force's remit was to, "assist the regular forces in time of tension and war, particularly in the guarding of vital United Kingdom installations".

The four pilot companies set up – based in Perth, Reading, Worcester and Bedfordshire/Hertfordshire – "quickly became very popular and grew rapidly in personnel and in territory". As before, wildly over-ambitious aims were declared, the objective being to raise a total of 50,000 men and women. In fact, by 1985, more than 50 Home Service Force squadrons or companies had been formed. The force was never called into action and, with the ending of the Cold War, it was disbanded in 1992, finally ending a legacy of voluntary service that stretched back to the dark days of the summer of 1940.

NOTES

1. David Carroll, *Dad's Army* (Sutton, Stroud, 2002), p.113.
2. *Hansard*, House of Commons Debate, March 15, 1955 vol 538 cc1220-34.

Global Citizenship

Education for Social Justice

Dr Wendy Booth

A textbook for Secondary Schools

Promotes an understanding of social dynamics and structural inequalities

Addresses the core principles of citizenship education

Contains classroom activities

Relevant to the Sustainable Development Goals

Preface

Our Team

Dr Wendy Booth works as a Lecturer in Public Service Management and is Course Leader for Sociology at the University of South Wales within the Social Policy Research Team. She has conducted extensive research into racism and ethno-cultural empathy, and issues related to class and life chances.
Katie Derradji-Brown has an MEd in Education and her research focused on the United Nations' 17 Goals for Sustainable Development in relation to teaching and pedagogy. Sustainability Sphere is their combined effort to make a difference to citizens and the planet.

Our Aim

The aim of the resources produced by Sustainability Sphere is to provide children and young people with knowledge and awareness of the social aspect of sustainability and the climate change emergency we are facing, to encourage them to become responsible citizens of the world.

Our recommended activities support children in thinking about the impact of their own and others' actions, encouraging them to become empathetic, caring individuals. They should realise how, through creativity and critical thinking, they can find solutions to problems to help humanity and the planet.

Aim & Learning Objectives

The aim of this textbook is to explore global citizenship in relation to social justice and the treatment and life chances of others. The information and practical classroom activities support the structuring of lessons that encourage learners to be global citizens of the world who are empathic and tolerant of others.

The first section discusses prejudice and racism from different angles to show how and why it occurs; the impact it has, and what can be done about it. The second section focuses on inequalities and how social class and geographies affect people's life chances. Sociological theories and social psychology form the pedagogical basis, and critical thinking skills and self reflection are encouraged throughout.

Learning Objectives:

- To consider examples of stereotyping and the impact stereotyping has
- To differentiate between prejudiced thoughts and racist actions
- To recognise the impact of racism on groups of people and individuals
- To develop ways of addressing racism through creative tasks and critical thinking
- To create awareness of how we label others and the impact that can have
- To learn about and research key figures related to Black and ethnic minority history
- To understand how in-groups and out-groups form
- To engage in self-reflection while considering migration and other countries and cultures
- To explore the advantages of living in a diverse society
- To recognise various forms of inequalities
- To realise that inequalities are often beyond the control of the person suffering
- To consider the reasons why people migrate
- To explore different types of inequality, such as social class and gender
- To examine the geographical aspect of inequalities, including the north-south divide
- To problem solve and consider solutions to inequalities
- To consider who is responsible and how to take action

Contents

This textbook addresses the following SDGs:

PART 1: PREJUDICE & RACISM

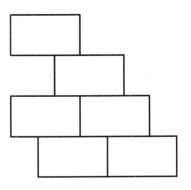

A reminder to be kind and think good of others:
"If a person has ugly thoughts, it begins to show on the
face. And when that person has ugly thoughts every
day, every week, every year, the face gets uglier and
uglier until you can hardly bear to look at it.

A person who has good thoughts cannot ever be ugly.
You can have a wonky nose and a crooked mouth and
a double chin and stick-out teeth, but if you have good
thoughts it will shine out of your face like sunbeams
and you will always look lovely."

(Roald Dahl, The Twits)

Beginning to Think Critically

These introductory pages support critical thinking by encouraging learners to reflect on how stereotyping occurs, and why we make assumptions about others

Stereotyping

Stereotyping involves having a belief about a certain group of individuals and assuming that every member of that group is the same. When we meet someone for the first time, we look at their main characteristic, known as their 'master status', and this affects our initial thoughts about them.

Can you think of any examples of Stereotyping? Look at the pictures for clues.
Do you agree that we do this?
What is the problem with stereotyping?

Stereotyping: Examples

Look at this photograph of a guitarist. What springs to mind when you look at him?

Look at this photograph of a man who arrived in the UK as refugee from Somalia. What springs to mind about him?

Perhaps you assumed the guitar player was not interested in getting an education and the refugee is poor and may be out of work and isolated.

In reality, the guitar player is the famous Brian May from the rock band Queen, and he has a PhD in Astrophysics. The man who arrived as a refugee is Magid Magid, and he was the Lord Mayor of Sheffield from 2018 to 2019.

The initial ideas that came into your mind are stereotypes - the images that pop into your head when you think of a person or group of people. It is normal for things to spring to mind when we meet people, but we must be careful that they do not effect our attitude and behaviour towards them.

Prejudice & Discrimination

Stereotyping leads to prejudice, and acting on it is discrimination

Key Terms

Prejudice: An attitude (often based on stereotyping) which makes us think in a favourable or unfavourable way towards a specific group. It can be positive or negative, though it is usually associated with negative feelings.

Discrimination: is when we act upon these thoughts or feelings.

Think of an example of prejudice, and then an act of discrimination based on that prejudice.

Positive Discrimination: often used as a 'tool' to re-balance discrimination (e.g. attempts to employ more ethnic minority police officers, or guaranteeing that job applicants with a disability are shortlisted for interview).

What is Racism?

Racism is someone behaving differently towards another person based on the colour of their skin or culture.
Some people believe that they are better than other people just because of the colour of their skin or because of the country they are from.

Some people are bullied because they look different, speak a different language, have a different accent, wear different clothes, eat different food, or have a different religion.
In Western countries, a lot of racism comes from history and colonialism, because White Europeans were in charge of a lot of countries around the world, and they thought they were better than the people who lived there. This led to 'White culture' becoming normal and seen as good, with other cultures seen as different and inferior.
There are other types of racism within other countries and cultures, but it is always based on seeing others as different and inferior.

___

Questions
1. Why are some people racist?

2. What are some of the differences between people?

3. What happened in history that led to racism?

Racism on the Buses

Racial discrimination led to the Bristol Bus Boycott of 1963. The Bristol Omnibus Company refused to employ Black or Asian bus drivers, which was unfair and made people angry, so they boycotted the company by refusing to travel on their buses. Students from Bristol University held a protest march, and some famous politicians spoke out about the bus company. On the 28th of August 1963, the bus company announced that there would be no more discrimination, and soon after, the UK government passed the Race Relations Act, which made racial discrimination in public places unlawful.

Task: Design a slogan for the side of the bus to encourage people not to be prejudiced or racist.

Unequal Treatment due to Racism

Even though racism is unlawful, it still happens, but is sometimes hard to prove. For example:

- Black people in England and Wales are 40 times more likely than White people to be stopped and searched by the police
- In the UK, Black people are more than twice as likely to die in police custody
- In the US, Black people are five times as likely as White people to go to prison
- Workers in some countries are exploited because they are from poor backgrounds
- During the Covid 19 pandemic, people from ethnic minorities in the UK were more likely to die, espcially health-workers such as doctors, and those providng essential services, such as bus drivers.

Racism is the reason for the Black Lives Matter protests that have been taking place all over the world. In 2020, the Black Lives Matter movement gained momentum after the death of George Floyd in the US.

Task: Independent Research
What happened to Breonna Taylor and Mark Duggan?
What was the public and the media's reaction?

When Things Go Wrong

Stephen Lawrence was an 18 year old Black man from London. In April 1993, he was waiting at a bus stop when he was racially attacked and killed by a gang of White youths. Because of racism, the police did not properly investigate the murder, and Stephen's family fought for justice for many years. They helped to highlight the impact from racism within the police force.

The Covid 19 pandemic started in Wuhan in China in 2019. Since the start of the pandemic, people from China and East Asia have been insulted and attacked by people blaming them for the pandemic; even though it has nothing to do with them!

The Black Lives Matter protests started after the death of George Floyd who was killed by a police officer in the US after he was arrested and restrained outside a shop. People were already angry at the unfair treatment of Black people, and his death sparked protests.

Racism can be overcome: This photograph shows a White man who was hurt at a protest. The Black man is Patrick Hutchinson, and he explained how, "His life was under threat, so I just went under, scooped him up, put him on my shoulders and started marching towards the police with him."

Photograph from The Guardian 14/06/20

Task

Imagine someone new is starting your school or club, or visiting your home.

Answer the following questions:

How can you make them feel welcome?

What will you ask them?

How will you communicate if they don't speak much English?

What will you do if someone else behaves in a racist way towards them?

Try reversing the questions by imagining you are the new person - how would you like to be treated?

LABELLING THEORY

Match the label to the animal:

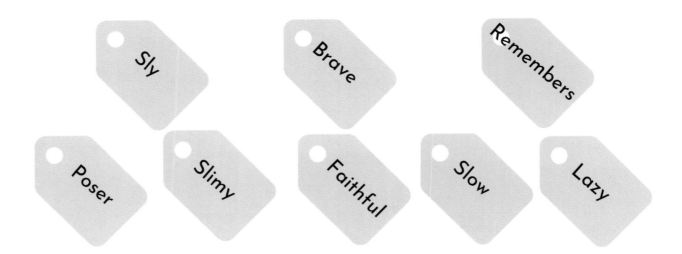

Sly

Brave

Remembers

Poser

Slimy

Faithful

Slow

Lazy

On the previous page, you put labels on different animals. Sometimes, people give other people labels too!
Is this right or wrong? Let's think about it. Look at the diagram below which shows an example from school about how a student can be given a label..

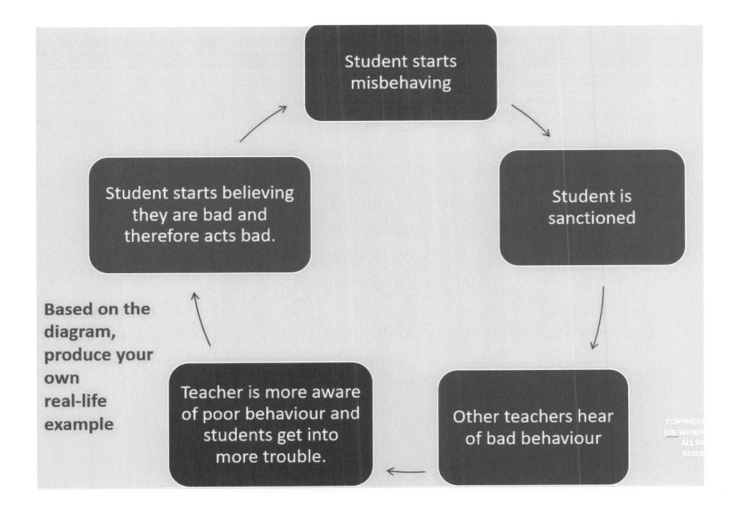

Based on the diagram, produce your own real-life example

The impact from labelling is enormous. The educational psychologists, Rosenthal and Jacobson, found that when teachers believe that a child is less intelligent (even if it is not true), they will treat him or her like that, and the child will end up with worse grades - not because he or she lacks the skills needed, but because he or she has received less attention from the teacher.

Have you ever felt labelled?
Have you ever noticed a friend being labelled?
How did that make you feel?

Toni Morrison, an American author who won the Nobel Prize for Literature, wrote: "the definitions belong to the definitors, not to the defined."
What do you think she means?

How will you react if someone tries to label you? Will you 'believe' them?

Extension Activity: What will the impact of labelling be if a child is negatively labelled throughout school?

Re-considering Labelling

Sometimes when we label people, we lower our expectations of them, and this can lead to people lowering their expectations of themselves, and not believing they can do well. Many people have not done as well as they could, or have made poor life choices, because of not being helped and supported due to being labelled (e.g. not being put in high achieving groups in school, not being given good jobs, not being promoted at work, and not being welcomed by important groups in society such as political parties).

We see this all around us, but there are exceptions, and the following pages focus on positive examples of where people have refused to believe their label and have succeeded. Reading about these examples should help us not to judge others, and if we feel we are being labelled negatively, it should help us not to accept that label. This is why it is important for stories to be told, and for voices to be heard.

Task: Think of someone you admire. Write about why you admire them

Extension Activity: Consider whether the person you admire may have been labelled, and what might have happened if they were labelled.

Gladys West: A Real-life Example

- Gladys West is a Black lady who grew up on a farm in the US.
- Gladys was determined to get a good education because she didn't want to work on the farm.
- She worked so hard in school that she won a scholarship to university, and she worked as a babysitter to earn money to pay her rent.
- Gladys went on to do a Masters in Mathematics.
- She then got a job at a naval base working as a programmer and doing coding on the huge computing machines.
- Gladys rose through the ranks, and along with her team, she laid the groundwork for modern GPS.
- So, when you use a SatNav, remember the hard work of Gladys West.

Discuss, or write down, what you think
made Gladys West succeed.

Tanni Grey-Thompson

- Tanni Grey-Thompson was born with spina bifada, but she didn't let that stop her.
- Her parents fought for her to go to a mainstream school instead of a special school, and eventually the local authority agreed.
- While at school, Tanni Grey-Thompson realised that she enjoyed sport, especially wheelchair racing.
- She went on to become a paralympian and won 1 bronze, 4 silver and 11 gold medals.
- Tanni Grey-Thompson did a degree in Politics and Social Administration, and she is now a Peer in the House of Lords, with the title Baroness.
- She is married with a daughter.

Discuss, or write down, what qualities helped
Tanni Grey-Thompson to be so successful.

Nelson Mandela: A Real-life Example

- Nelson Mandela was born in South Africa in 1918.
- He studied hard at school and studied Law at university.
- South Africa was made up of so many different races that it was called the rainbow nation.
- However, there was a system of apartheid in South Africa, which meant that Black and White people had to stay separate. The White people had good jobs and went to good schools, whereas the Black people were stuck in poverty.
- Nelson Mandela fought apartheid by joining a political party that was against apartheid, and even helped to build an army to overthrow the apartheid government.
- In 1962, Nelson Mandela was arrested for this, and he spent 27 years in prison.
- Nelson Mandela never gave up, and there is a song called Free Nelson Mandela, which became popular around the world.
- In 1990, Nelson Mandela was set free from prison, and he worked with the South African government on ending apartheid.
- In 1994, Nelson Mandela was voted president of South Africa – he was the country's first Black president.

Discuss, or list, what you think made Nelson Mandela succeed.

Research Task

Choose one or more of the following people and find out what they were famous for:

Martin Luther King

Muhammed Ali

Maya Angelou

Benjamin Zephaniah

CV Raman

Louis Braille

Ibn Sina (Avicenna)

Barak Obama

Tim Jenkin

Mansa Musa

Madam C J Walker

Rosa Parks

Abdul Karim CVO

Stephen Hawking

Jing Fang

Betty Campbell

Toni Morrison

John Alcindor

Mary Seacole

Write a diary entry pretending to be the person you have researched. Think about what happened that day, the people you saw, and your plans for the future.

GAL

What are your goals for next month, next year, in ten years?
Write a list.

How will you achieve those goals? Will you need help? If so, who
from?

Draw a diagram showing your plan, or write two paragraphs
about your goals.

Reach for the stars

In-groups & Out-groups

Important concept: In-group against Out-group

A famous psychologist called Henri Tajfel found that being in a group can cause prejudice towards those in other groups.

He also found that we tend to prefer our own group over others, and we make excuses for the mistakes of the people in our own group, but are less forgiving towards people in other groups.

Some examples of groups are sports teams; music and book fans; collectors; speakers of the same language; people from the same country or culture; followers of certain fashions.

Are you in any groups?

How do you feel about that?

Do you do more to support the people in your own group?

In-groups & Out-group: Examples

In an experiment on Man United and Liverpool football fans, they were more likely to help someone who fell over if they were wearing the same football shirt as them!

Check the news for stories involving in-groups and out-groups, for example football supporters or political parties.

OR:

Discuss fictional stories such as vampires and werewolves; Pikachu and Bulbasaur, or Gryffindor and Slytherin.

Take some Picts, Celts and Silures
And let them settle,
Then overrun them with Roman conquerors.

Remove the Romans after approximately 400 years
Add lots of Norman French to some
Angles, Saxons, Jutes and Vikings, then stir vigorously.

Mix some hot Chileans, cool Jamaicans, Dominicans,
Trinidadians and Bajans with some Ethiopians, Chinese,
Vietnamese and Sudanese.

Then take a blend of Somalians, Sri Lankans, Nigerians
And Pakistanis,
Combine with some Guyanese
And turn up the heat.

Sprinkle some fresh Indians, Malaysians, Bosnians,
Iraqis and Bangladeshis together with some
Afghans, Spanish, Turkish, Kurdish, Japanese
And Palestinians
Then add to the melting pot.

Leave the ingredients to simmer.

As they mix and blend allow their languages to flourish
Binding them together with English.

Allow time to be cool.

Add some unity, understanding, and respect for the future,
Serve with justice
And enjoy.

Note: All the ingredients are equally important. Treating one
ingredient better than another will leave a bitter unpleasant taste.

The poem on the previous page is called The British; it was written by a famous Black poet called Benjamin Zephaniah.

In the poem, he mentions some people from history, such as the Saxons and Romans - why is that?

Why do you think he describes people in the poem as if something is cooking?

What lesson can we learn from the poem?

Write your own poem about people and the world.
Think about:
The history of the people where you live.
Any countries you would like to visit
Countries or places you've been to (this can be in your own town or city)
The sights, sounds, colours, smells, atmosphere etc

Citizens of the World

Use an atlas/world map that show the countries of the world (either a book or online).

Write a list of the countries you have seen in films or documentaries.

Think about the different food you eat - look up the countries it is from.

Think about fruit and vegetables - list which countries they are from.

Do you have friends from different countries? If so, write them down too and look at pictures of those countries.

Have you been to any other countries? What was it like?

Would you like to visit a different country or countries? If so, why?

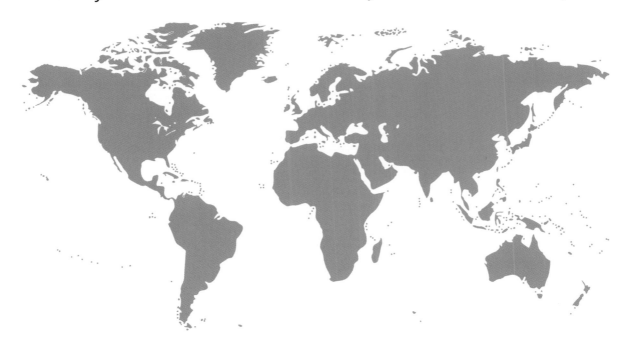

Make an information leaflet about your favourite country.

Ideas: Japan; Italy; Dubai; the Amazon; pineapples; chocolate; noodles; curry; safari; scuba diving; Mount Everest; rugby; football; dolphins; sharks; falcons; music

Diverse Citizens

Think about the advantages of knowing lots of different people and experiencing different things from different cultures.

Fill in the boxes below with some positive things about diversity.

Things I like about diversity

Watch the Channel 4 television show 'How the Other Kids Live.'

Think about what information you could put in a poster to tell people to stop being racist and to encourage diversity. Draw a mind map of ideas.

Make a poster on diversity.
Use pens, pencils or paints, or design the poster on your computer.

Extension Activity: Write about your poster and why you choose the words and design.

Book Review

Read one of the books below, or one similar, and write a review on it:

- Windrush Child by Benjamin Zephaniah
- The Lion Above the Door by Onjali Rauf
- Refugee by Alan Gratz
- Coming to England by Floella Benjamin (younger)
- To Kill a Mocking Bird by Harper Lee (older)

Title:

Author:

What is the book about?

Would you recommend the book? Why?

What ages and interests is the book suitable for?

And finally...

Write a letter to your local MP, head teacher or someone important, about the problem of racism and what you think should be done about it. Include some of the main ideas you have learnt from these resources.

Remember, most people are kind like the description in the poem by Roald Dahl on the first page, but if you feel upset by what you have learnt, make sure you chat to a teacher, family member or friend about it.

Part Two: Inequalities & Life Chances

INEQUALITIES

The variations in wealth and consumption patterns around the world highlight the extent of inequalities, providing a solid starting point for exploring this topic and supporting critical thinking. As in the previous section, there are tasks for learners throughout.

The Haves & The Have Nots

There are lots of types of inequalities and reasons why people are not treated the same as others. Some inequalities are based on our background and where we live. There are poor people and rich people everywhere, but overall, some countries have much more than others.

How many planet earths do we need?

While in areas of some countries people are struggling even to get enough to eat, in other countries, people's lifestyles are having a negative impact on the world. According to overshoot.org, the lifestyles and consumption of people in some countries means we would need even more planet earths if everyone lived like that!
The table below shows how many planet earths a variety of countries need to maintain their current lifestyles:

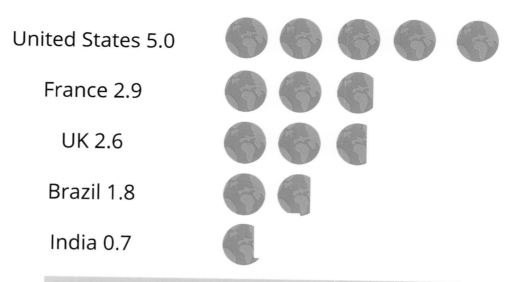

United States 5.0

France 2.9

UK 2.6

Brazil 1.8

India 0.7

Question: What do you think? Is this fair? Why?

30

WEALTH, RESOURCES & POVERTY

Relative poverty is when a person does not have the minimum standard of living when compared to others living in the same place.

Abject poverty is when people do not have even basic needs, including food, safe drinking water, shelter, healthcare and education.

When we think about wealth and resources, we usually consider how much money people have. This is important, but the impact of wealth and resources is much greater than whether someone can afford the latest television or trainers. In addition, if people living in abject poverty manage to improve their situation and gain more wealth and resources, the impact of living in poverty is still likely to affect them for the rest of their lives.

Challenge: In what ways will living in poverty affect someone? Even if it is temporary and their life changes

Cultural Capital

Cultural capital refers to our social relationships, including norms such as manners and customs, and language and the way we speak. It is related to how we behave, dress and interact with others. Sometimes we are expected to behave a certain way in order to fit in, and our background has an impact on this. For example, someone who has gone to a public (private fee paying) school may enjoy rowing, polo and chess, and understand these hobbies, including the dress code and language, making it easier for them to fit in more with wealthy people. Regarding education, children who have had the opportunity to travel and visit museums may have a better understanding of history and geography. Therefore, economic capital, in particular money, affects our life experiences and cultural capital, as well as our ability to buy things.

Everyone has their own cultural capital. It can include knowledge of urban communities and how to interact 'on the street', or a culture's rich oral history. However, cultural capital is not valued equally in society, and it can cause deep social divides.

Think & discuss: What are the advantages of visiting places such as museums? Have you been to one, or is there a museum that you would like to visit?

Extension activity: Which universities did most UK politicians attend? Why? Do you think that is a good thing?

DIFFERENCES IN SOCIETY

Look at the pictures below:

What are they trying to tell us?

How do they make you feel?

Would you prefer to be rich or poor?

Why?

Challenge: What makes us happy that does not require money?

Extension activity: Write about a day or a week in the life of a poor person, and then do the same for a rich person. Read what you have written and consider what rich and poor actually mean. How much do we really need (or not need) to consider ourselves rich or poor?

There was once a businessman who was sitting by the beach in a small Brazilian village. As he sat, he saw a Brazilian fisherman rowing a small boat towards the shore having caught quite a few big fish. The businessman was impressed and asked the fisherman, "How long does it take you to catch so many fish?"

The fisherman replied, "Oh, just a short while."

"Then why don't you stay longer at sea and catch even more?" the businessman asked astonished.

"This is enough to feed my whole family," the fisherman said.

The businessman then asked, "So, what do you do for the rest of the day?"

The fisherman replied, "Well, I usually wake up early in the morning, go out to sea and catch a few fish, then go back and play with my kids. In the afternoon. I take a nap with my wife, and evening comes, I join my buddies in the village for a drink - we play guitar, sing and dance throughout the night."

The businessman offered a suggestion to the fisherman.

"I am a PhD in business management. I could help you to become a more successful person. From now on, you should spend more time at sea and try to catch as many fish as possible. When you have saved enough money, you could buy a bigger boat and catch even more fish. Soon you will be able to afford to buy more boats, set up your own company, your own production plant for canned food and a distribution network. By then, you will have moved out of this village and to Sao Paulo, where you can set up HQ to manage your other branches."

The fisherman continues, "And after that?"

The businessman laughs heartily, "After that, you can live like a king in your own house, and when the time is right, you can go public and float your shares on the Stock Exchange, and you will be rich."

The fisherman asks, "And after that?"

The businessman says, "After that, you can finally retire, you can move to a house by the fishing village, wake up early in the morning, catch a few fish, then return home to play with kids, have a nice afternoon nap with your wife, and when evening comes, you can join your buddies for a drink, play the guitar, sing and dance throughout the night!"

The fisherman was puzzled, "Isn't that what I am doing now?"

Activity

Draw your ideal home / life

What and who have you included and why?

MIGRATION

Simply put, migration means travelling to a new country. People have migrated for thousands of years for all sorts of reasons: to find new land (e.g. the Vikings); to trade (e.g. the Silk Route from Europe, through the Middle East to Asia); to flee famine and starvation (e.g. the Great Famine in the 1800s and Irish migration to America), and to avoid war (e.g. Syrian refugees fleeing to the UK).

Challenge: Where would you like to travel?
Discuss whether this is possible for you; are there any barriers?

The Windrush Generation

Sometimes those migrating are welcomed, and sometimes they are not. In the 1960s, Great Britain invited people from the Commonwealth, especially the Caribbean, to come to work in the UK in jobs such as nursing, public transport and in factories. They arrived on ships (the most famous one was called the Empire Windrush); however, even though the British government invited them, they were not welcomed by everyone and many found it difficult even to find a place to live.

Research: Look for information on the Windrush generation, including more recent news. Write a list to summarise what you have found out and you feel about it.

Extension Activity: Research: What is the Commonwealth?

IMMIGRATION: PUSH - PULL FACTORS

Push factors are why people leave a place (why they are pushed away), and pull factors are why people move to a place (what is pulling them there).

Label the following either push or pull factors:

- lack of healthcare (e.g. no hospitals)
- more wealth (e.g. more chance of education)
- high levels of crime (e.g. risk of being mugged)
- crop failure (so unable to feed family)
- flooding (e.g. homes washed away)
- high employment (so no jobs)
- better services (e.g. hospitals and schools)
- safety (e.g. no war or fighting)
- drought (no rain so no water to drink etc)
- less crime
- poverty (e.g. no money for food or education)
- political stability
- war
- less risk from natural hazards (e.g. flooding)

Some people are forced to move from their homes because of the push factors. They are often called refugees, asylum seekers or immigrants

Look online for poems about migration and refugees, for example **Home**, by the British-Somali poet Warsan Shire:

"no one leaves home unless home is the mouth of a shark."

What are the main topics/themes of these poems and how do they make you feel?

Extension activity: Write your own poem about migration. Think about themes such as war and danger; homesickness and meeting new people

Activity

Create two diary entries:

- One as a child or teenager in your own country about what happens when someone your own age arrives as a refugee in your street or school.

- One as a child or teenage refugee arriving in your country and starting your school or moving to live in your street.

Useful words:
Family, memories, strangers, language, skin colour, food, clothes, fear, sadness, smiles, loss, play games, anger, relief

Suggestions for extra reading:
Refugee by Alan Gratz
The Boy at the Back of the Class by Onjali Q Rauf

Draw a map of your local area that includes your home, the homes of people you visit, important facilities, and the places where you do your daily activities.

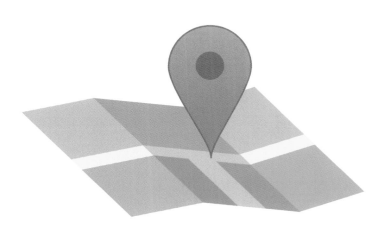

If you moved to a different country, which things on the map would you miss, and what would you try to do about it?

Extension activity: Put these things into order of priority and explain why some things are more important than others

40

SOCIAL CLASS: STILL A PROBLEM?

Classism means treating people differently based on their social class or perceived social class. It results in people from lower classes being disadvantaged and people from the middle class having more advantages. It is a huge problem because the gap between the rich and the poor is bigger than ever, and additional disadvantages are making things more difficult for those not born into wealthy, knowledgeable families. Classism can result in people not receiving access to the education and jobs they deserve.

Social class seems to affect different aspects of our lives - not just the job we do and the money we earn, but also our attitudes, lifestyles and values.

The billionnaire, Alan Sugar was recently criticised for posting a Tweet with a photograph of people in a plastic swimming pool, which he made fun of. It seemed to be an attack on working class people, and many on Twitter complained that a man who now owns a £12 million yacht had no right to post this.

What do you think?

Film & book suggestions:
Oliver Twist; Kes; Animal Farm

Careers

Social class is usually based on the person's career or job (or lack of work).

The National Statistics Socio-economic classification (NS-SEC) classifies occupations (jobs) to describe people's socio-economic position in society, and to explain differences in social behaviour and life chances. Those in jobs classed as higher level are likely to be paid more, be better educated, and have better health and live longer, than those in lower level jobs.

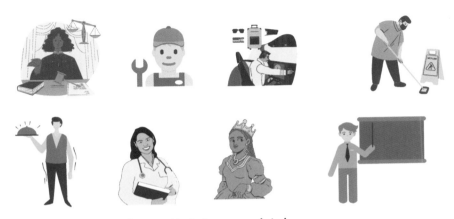

There are three main class divisions, which are:
working class (mainly manual workers);
middle class (people in professional jobs), and
upper class (e.g. executives and the aristocracy)

Put the pictures above into each of these categories.

... What about these people?

Wayne Rooni

J K Rowling

If you struggled with this and the previous task on careers - you are not alone - there is a lot of debate around the links between career, class and how much money people earn, and there are no definite right or wrong answers!

CLASS DIVIDES?

This is part of an article from The Guardian newspaper written by Dr Lisa McKenzie, the author of
Getting By, which discusses prejudice and stereotypes, and describes working-class life:

"The Sutton-in-Ashfield estate I grew up in, a mining town a few miles from Nottingham city centre, was a tight-knit community where almost everyone on the estate worked and lived in close proximity. I didn't know that we were no good; I didn't know that living on a council estate devalued you as a person. I understood my position in society as working class but I thought that was the best class to be. The middle class were boring, and the upper class were cruel – they hurt animals and sent their children away. This is how I thought about my family and my community during the 1970s. I was really thankful to be a working-class child.

During the late 1980s I felt very differently – almost ashamed of who we were. We were ridiculed, we were old-fashioned, poor, and didn't know what was happening in the cool world of the "yuppie" and "loadsamoney" – a catchphrase made up by a middle-class comedian about working class people made good."

Lisa McKenzie went on to do a degree in social work and a PhD and she is now a university lecturer, but she continues to be an activist for the working class.

Extension Activity: Make a list of bullet points on what the author sees as the good and bad points of being working class. Can you think of any more?

GENDER INEQUALITIES

"By denying women equal rights, we deny half the population a chance to live life at its fullests" (United Nations). Women did not always have the rights they have now, and women are still continuing the struggle.

Case Study: Emilie Kempin-Spyri

Emilie Kempin-Spyri was the first woman in Europe to gain a law degree in 1887; however, she was not allowed to have a career in law. Emile lived most of her life in Switzerland, but she moved to New York with her husband for a while where she set up a law school for women.
Emile was not allowed to teach in university because the male students and staff were against it.

Chaise Longue, University of Zurich

This is a chaise longue which is in the atrium of the University of Zurich in Switzerland - it is designed to remind people of Emile Kempin-Spyri and her struggle for women's rights. It is giant size as it is supposed to make us think of the phrase 'on the shoulders of giants.'
Why do you think that is?

What job do you want to do? Will your gender affect your plans?

 Recommended film: The Eagle Huntress

Things in Common

Write a list of things that everyone (or most people) value, and things that everyone (or most people) think are wrong.

1. _____
_____

2. _____
_____

3. _____
_____

4. _____
_____

5. _____
_____

6. _____
_____

THE NORTH-SOUTH DIVIDE

The countries that are shaded have an annual per head capita of less than 10,700 US dollars *GDP (PPP).
A low GDP means that a country is struggling to supply its people with everything they need. This may include food, clean water, energy (electricity and heating), and quality education.
Clearly then, the countries not shaded are richer - where are they mainly located on the map? Can you name any of the countries (either shaded or unshaded)?

*GDP: gross domestic product - measures the size of a country's economy
*PPP: purchasing power parity - takes into account the price of goods in a country
Map taken from the Royal Geographical Society

Variations in Wealth

Despite improvements around the world lifting millions of people out of absolute poverty, inequality between the world's richest and poorest countries is widening. There are many causes for these inequalities, for example, the availability of natural resources; variations in healthcare provision and education; the country's economy and industries; how countries are governed; conflict and war; climate change, and international trading policies which can restrict access to markets.

There are also large differences between rich and poor communities in the same countries, for example, while India has the highest number of poor people, it also has a very rich elite. Moreover, the richest 85 individual people in the world have the same amount of wealth as the poorest half of the whole world's population.

Is this fair? Why?

Extension Activity: Research the term 'social responsibility'

We must remember that it is impossible to judge a person's wealth (or education etc) by how they look or dress. The man on the right was flying first class, but the lady behind him told him he must be in the wrong queue because she assumed he couldn't afford it! The man, Emmit Walker, posted what happened on social media.

Emmit Walker

Between Country Differences

The poverty ratio is based on the percent of people living on less than 1.90 US Dollars a day. These are some examples for different countries using figures from 2018:

Angola 49.90

Laos 10

Brazil 4.40

Pakistan 4.40

Philippines 2.70

Romania 2.70

Mexico 1.70

Spain 0.90

Sweden 0.70

Poland 0.20

Greece 0.10

Russia 0

Turkey 0

Source: The World Bank

Plot a graph to show the differences between these countries

How much is $1.90 in your money (currency)?

Food Around the World

Thinking Task:

What do you eat on special occasions?

What did you eat today?

What did you eat yesterday?

Did you choose what you ate?

Was it healthy?

Did you enjoy it?

Did your friends and family eat the same things as you?

If not, why?

Research what families around the world eat. Create an online display of the different foods. What are the main differences between the countries on the map on the first page in this section?

World Food

Food Poverty

One in nine people around the world are hungry or undernourished. This leads to health problems and difficulty fighting off illness and disease.

How do you feel when you are hungry? Do you feel like doing your homework or helping out with housework?

Food poverty can be caused by financial poverty, food shortages, climate change, food waste, lack of government support, war, and migration.

This plant is called enset (also known as false banana). It is used in Ethiopia to make porridge and bread, and scientists believe it could be grown across Africa to boost food security (to make sure everyone is fed).

Enset

Try making porridge. Do you like it? Would you like to eat it twice every day? Can you add anything to give it variety (e.g. honey, fruit...)? Think about enset as a solution to food poverty.

Food poverty doesn't just affect people in poorer countries. Sometimes we all need support, such as getting food from a food bank, so let's all be kind and generous, as we never know when we will need a bit help.

POSSIBLE SOLUTIONS

You have learnt that there are wide differences in how much wealth people around the world have, which affects what they eat, their desire to travel and their life chances (health, education and career). It is important for us to think about how this can be addressed.

Project: Choose an activity that will help to make a difference. This may be: donating to a food bank or other charity; doing volunteer work such as making up food parcels; posting information online or making an information poster, or writing to a politician or other famous person.

Write a diary entry about your project.

Think about:

- How it went
- If it will have an impact
- Why you chose to do it
- Whether you would like to do something else in the future

WHO'S RESPONSIBLE?

Who is responsible for inequalities and life chances in society?
You made a difference with your project, but what can be
done on a larger scale?

Making choices: if you had to choose between food, heating your house
or paying for your education, what would you choose?

CASE STUDY:
ANEURIN BEVAN

Aneurin Bevan was one of the most important politicians in the Labour Party after the Second World War.

Aneurin Bevan was born into a poor, working class mining family in the Welsh Valleys in 1897, and so he was very aware of poverty, ill health and disease.

He left school at age 13, but he later won a scholarship and went to study in London, eventually becoming a politician.

When Labour came to power in 1945, Aneurin Bevan was appointed Minister of Health. Britain had been through a terrible time during the war, and leaders of all political parties wanted to build a better country for the people. Aneurin Bevan was passionate about his role and the health of the population, and he was responsible for establishing the National Health Service (the NHS), allowing free medical services and treatment for everyone in the UK for the first time.

Can you think of any other people (nowadays or from history) who have done their best to help others?

And finally...

Which part of this section do you remember the most?

Will this affect your role as a citizen of the world in any way in the future?

Extension activity: Write a speech about your thoughts on inequalities and fairness

Thank you for choosing Sustainability Sphere©

Look out for more resources and information at:
https://sustainability-sphere.com/

Follow us on social media at:
https://www.instagram.com/sustainability.sphere/

Email us at:
sustainability.sphere@gmail.com

Managed and Produced by:
Dr Wendy A Booth and Katie Brown BSc

Printed in Great Britain
by Amazon